MAKE AMERICA SANE AGAIN

MAKE AMERICA SANE AGAIN

REFLECTIONS ON TRUMP'S TRAVESTIES

SHELDON HIRSCH

FIRST HILL BOOKS

FIRST HILL BOOKS
An imprint of Wimbledon Publishing Company Limited (WPC)

This edition first published in UK and USA 2026
by FIRST HILL BOOKS
75–76 Blackfriars Road, London SE1 8HA, UK
or PO Box 9779, London SW19 7ZG, UK
and
244 Madison Ave #116, New York, NY 10016, USA

British Library Cataloguing-in-Publication Data
A catalogue record for this book is available from the British Library.

Library of Congress Control Number: 2026932815

ISBN-13: 978-1-83999-949-9
ISBN-10: 1-83999-949-7

Cover image credit: Easy-Peasy.AI

This title is also available as an eBook.

CONTENTS

ACKNOWLEDGMENTS

I am grateful to many people who helped with this book.

To my wife Linda, our children Robert, Jackie, and Richard, and our son-in-law Danny, for being great people and, each in their own way, very supportive.

To Arnie Berns, a fabulous nephrologist who kindled my own interest in nephrology, hired me to join his practice, mentored me for over thirty years, and has always been a good friend. Arnie turned out to be an equally talented editor, a real Renaissance man. He read every sentence of this book and improved many of them. Great job, Arnie!

To three other great physicians, friends, and readers, who provided great cheer and support: Bob Cohen, David Goldfarb, and Jerry Osher.

To my brother Alan, another Renaissance man who helped with this project.

Thank you to all.

INTRODUCTION

This book describes my personal (written) battle against Donald Trump, his assault on democracy, and other Trump-related calamities.

No one who knows me would ever have thought, until recently, that I would write a book with any connection to politics. For most of my life, I identified with the party of apathy, a political agnostic. I grew up in an apolitical household. Not totally, as my mother and father were devoted to Israel. But they were just one-issue voters and I don't think we ever talked American politics at home.

I do remember going to a Nixon rally in 1968 when I was 13 years old and chanting "four more years" along with the adoring crowd. However, I did not know anything about Nixon or his policies; I just went along with some friends for fun. As soon as I left, I forgot about Nixon and all of it.

I had no political affiliations or interests in college. I did vote for the first time in 1976, for Gerald Ford, but that was because he seemed a nice guy and was an ex-football player, which, as a huge football fan, seemed cool to me. In retrospect, I am not proud of that reasoning. For the rest of my adult life, I voted equally between Democrats and Republicans, and sometimes nobody, and it was almost always based on personality and/or character, not issues.

I disliked Bill Clinton and Al Gore, so I voted Republican three times in a row. Then I voted for John Kerry over George Bush, and that was based on an actual issue—Bush's mishandling of the Iraq War. After that, I too got caught up in Barack Obama's charisma and voted for him twice.

That brings me to the 2016 election, Hillary Clinton versus Trump. I didn't like Hillary any more than I liked Bill, so I would not vote for her. But I could not bring myself to actually vote for Trump, not after all his relentlessly childish behavior and his absurd public slur directed at Carly Fiorina. I addressed that dilemma by not voting, but rooting for Trump. I was pleased with his victory.

What then happened to change me from "pleased with Trump's victory" to a "Never Trumper"? Lots of things, of course, but there were four important "lowlights" in his first term. To use medical jargon, my transition was "evidence-based."

First, on day one, we witnessed Trump's delusional, paranoid, narcissistic, dishonest shenanigans with his inauguration photo. That told me his preelection craziness was real, not a posture. Still, this was just words, which, as it turned out, would become an occasional defense of Trump, roughly, "yes, he's a bad person and he says ridiculous things and lies all the time, but the words don't translate into action, and he's great on the issues." Well, at that early time, he had not yet hurt anyone as president, so day one did not turn me against him as much as put me on alert that my previous thinking was naive and the future was worrisome.

But then we saw the separation of children from their families at the southern border, with many children reportedly put in cages. Who does this to children? What did this say about Trump that he allowed this, and for so long?

And, again putting to the test the question of whether his words mattered, the COVID-19 pandemic arrived.

COVID-19 receives a lot of attention in this book in part, because as a doctor, I was personally involved. But also, because this was the litmus test of Trump's first term. How would he perform as our national leader in a crisis? Trump's performance was so harmful that it put a conclusive lie to "words do not matter." People died because of him! Similarly, I devote a later chapter to RFK Jr.'s appointment, both out of my personal interest as a physician and because as COVID-19 defined Trump's major failure in his first term, RFK Jr.'s appointment is one of his major failures early on in his second term.

Finally, the Jan. 6 insurrection. What could be worse than one man summoning a crowd to attempt to thwart a lawful presidential transition and to insert, instead, an unelected person to rule the country? And it came so close to succeeding!

Thus, by the end of his term, the psychiatric/psychological disturbances evident on Day One had manifested catastrophically, and to great damage.

In my eventual disdain for Trump, I joined the Lincoln Project and the scores of noted life-long Republicans—including Michael Steele (ex-chair of the Republican National Committee), various senators and congressman, many of his first term appointees (Bolton, Kelly, Mathis, McMaster, etc.), famous conservative writers (French, Frum, Goldberg, Kagan, and many more), White House Officials (Cobb, Griffin, Grisham, Hutchison, Mathews, among others), President Bush, Vice President Cheney [...] I'll stop there.

After the Jan 6 disaster, Trump seemed toast, as virtually everyone from both parties properly excoriated him. But that did not last long. Just a month later, Republican Speaker of the House Kevin McCarthy traveled to Trump's home, as if McCarthy was the one asking for forgiveness. And Trump ended up, once again, as the Republican candidate for president.

I had written a few letters to newspapers about him prior to that, but as Trump rose like a phoenix, I started writing more regularly. Almost all to the *New York Times* or *Chicago Tribune*, and almost all in response to something Trump did or said that day or someone else said about what Trump did or said that day. This seemed like a way that a kidney doctor, completely removed from politics, could add to the Trump resistance, even if just a little. It struck me as my civic duty.

After Trump was reelected and his agenda put into place piece by piece, the pace of the letters accelerated—there was so much more to fight for.
Eleven of the first batch of letters were published, a rate much higher than the industry standard, which gave me a jolt of positive feedback; that maybe I had something worthwhile to say. Eventually, I realized that I had sent enough letters, published and unpublished, to comprise an easily readable, fast-paced book, documenting Trump's travesties as they unfolded, often on a daily basis. That is what this book is: A compilation of my thoughts about Trump and his failings, all in real time as they happened.

With that, please start turning the pages.

PART ONE

Trump's First Term

CHAPTER 1

FIRST TERM DEBACLES

January 25, 2017
Trump's Inauguration Crowd: When Someone Shows You Who They Are, Believe Them
Dear Editors,

I was pleased with Donald Trump's election victory based on my "ABC viewpoint": Anyone But Clinton. But with reservations. Most of the time during the campaign, Trump behaved like a spoiled child and/or a schoolyard bully—I mean, puerile nicknames for respected political figures? Worst of all, his utterly obnoxious and misogynist comment about the accomplished female presidential candidate Carly Fiorina: "Look at that face. Would anyone vote for that?" I should have thought, who would vote for anyone who would say that? What decent and mature person says something that mean, childish, and pointless, especially on a national stage?

However, perhaps due to the abiding and persuasive power of "ABC," I rationalized it. It seemed like Trump was not really taking his campaign too seriously, at least not in the usual fashion. In the beginning, he seemed to have no chance of winning and was in it for a lark, a fun time for a bored billionaire. Or simply a means to increase name brand in the interests of cashing in; after all, making money was his lifetime passion. I assumed that if Trump beat Clinton, got slapped in the face with "OMG, I am the President of the United States," he would instantly get serious, rid himself of all the meanness and childishness, and start behaving like a president. In that case, we would have someone who had sold himself as super-smart, super-accomplished, with different and favorable experiences and perspectives, and who had jettisoned his baggage.

However, there was reason to doubt that construct. He had gone to Wharton Undergraduate School, not the esteemed Wharton Business School as he routinely implied, and he had threatened lawsuits to prevent the release of his grades. His business history included a slew of bankruptcies and failures, not a story of brilliance and unmitigated success, but the mantra of "Anyone But Clinton" impaired my thinking.

Then came day one of his presidency—DAY ONE—and Trump told me that I had missed the boat. I refer specifically to White House press secretary Sean Spicer's insistence—prompted and reinforced by Trump—that Trump's inauguration crowd was not only larger than Obama's, but the largest ever, despite clear photographic evidence to the contrary. This made me wonder: What kind of man fixates on his crowd size? Seemingly, a small and narcissistic man. And, if he believed what he was saying, add paranoid and delusional.

Then, at Trump's direction, the White House sent out obviously cropped photographs to supposedly buttress his point. So, we can add dishonest to the mix. What other explanation is there?

If the sequence of lies and/or delusions seems inconsequential [...] per se, yes, but not for what it revealed about Trump.

In a jiffy, I have gone from happy about Trump's election to very concerned.

As Maya Angelou said, "When someone shows you who they are, believe them."

———————

July 30, 2017
Obamacare: That Can Not Be Allowed
Dear Editors,

Senator John McCain's thumbs-down vote essentially put President Trump's and the Republican Party's fevered quest to end the Affordable Care Act (ACA) on death's row.

McCain's nay vote is commonly misunderstood. It did not support the ACA—this was not a vote on the ACA—"repeal with no replacement" had already been voted down. It also was not a vote on the Republican's own healthcare plan, termed The Better Care Reconciliation Act (BCRA); that, too, had been voted down in the Senate. This was a vote on a scaled-down BCRA, a skinny bill, that was not going to be, even if McCain voted thumbs-up, the law of the land. Since it was a new bill, it would have had to go back to the House for approval. And everyone understood it would not be approved by the House, since it was too scaled down. But that was not the point of it, which was simply to keep the process alive, to give the House another chance—a redo—to come up with a decent bill to send back to the Senate.

McCain explained his thinking as "Skinny repeal fell short because it fell short of our promise to repeal and replace Obamacare with meaningful reform."

That seemed carefully non-offensive, particularly as his action seemed to say, "Enough of this sad story, we've had seven years to come up with a decent plan to replace the ACA and if we're back to square zero after seven years, time to move on." That certainly was the effect of McCain's no vote—end of story, move on.

The ACA was a Trump/Republican bête noire, after all, how could they fail at something so important to them?

The benign explanation was best offered, sort of, by Trump, "Nobody knew health care could be so complicated." Actually, everyone knew, except him. Health care in this country is complicated and difficult, and it was no surprise the Republicans could not come up with something better than the ACA.

A less benign view of the Republican failure notes that Trump and his Republican colleagues did not bother to come up with anything concrete until seven years after the ACA passed. They just name-called and predicted disasters. Trump certainly had no idea; his campaign promise was along the lines of "We'll come up with something." In the end, they failed to find anything and were obviously groping. Actually, improving health care seemed out of reach and not even a priority for them; all that mattered was eliminating the ACA.

Why the mania about eliminating the ACA? After all, it provided health insurance (and improved health) to millions, and without incurring a single one of the Armageddon-like horrors, Trump and the Republicans insisted would surely follow.

The ACA is a successful Obama and Democrat legislation, approved by the general public, and gaining in popularity over the last couple of years. Trump could not abide that.

In the Trump worldview, when your enemy succeeds, you fail, and that is just not allowed.

May 9, 2018
Trump Annuls Iran Nuclear Deal: Subtraction by Subtraction
Dear Editors,

Yesterday, President Trump announced the U.S. withdrawal from the Joint Comprehensive Plan of Action (JCPOA), known as the Iran nuclear deal. This had been negotiated by President Obama to prevent Iran from producing nuclear weapons.

JCPOA was implemented in January 2016. Iran agreed to reduce its stockpile of uranium and plutonium—below the enrichment level needed to create a bomb—and reduce its number of centrifuges, redesign several facilities for civilian uses, and allow robust monitoring, verification, and inspection from the International Atomic Energy Agency (IAEA). Subsequently, the IAEA confirmed Iran's compliance. As a result, the time Iran needed to build a nuclear weapon had increased from an estimated two to three months to more than 12 months.

Trump's complete withdrawal is problematic. If he felt that the JCPOA was lacking—and surely no agreement is beyond criticism—or that Iran was covertly skirting the agreement, and presumably they were, common sense dictates that one should renegotiate and improve the agreement, while keeping in place those aspects that were serving their purpose.

Instead, Trump simply burned it down and returned to square one. He reinstituted sanctions, but basically, his plan, as stated, is aspirational: "President Trump will work to assemble a broad coalition of nations to deny Iran all paths to a nuclear weapon and to counter the totality of the regime's malign activities." In other words, he is hoping for the best.

The burning down without replacement is so reckless that it suggests some unstated motivation. An obvious explanation would be that the JCPOA (like the ACA, which Trump has also tried to eliminate) is a signature President Obama accomplishment; Obama getting credit for anything good rankles Trump no end. That possibility is suggested by Trump's pointless name-calling, obviously intended at Obama, "The Iran Deal was one of the worst and most one-sided transactions the United States has ever entered into." If you don't like Obama, then you don't like his deals.

Trump better be able to deliver or else American and world safety has just taken a huge leap backward. At this time, we've lost restrictions on Iran and gained absolutely nothing.

This might be called "subtraction by subtraction."

———————————

June 22, 2018
Separating Children From Their Mothers. Yes, We Did
Dear Editors,

President Trump recently signed an executive order that ended the separation of children from their parents at the southern border. This is cause for celebration. By some estimates, as many as 5,000 children were separated from their parents with no tracking process instituted to allow their eventual return.

However, this raises multiple important questions, including:

How did this catastrophe take place?
Why did it take so long for President Trump to end it?
Why is there no provision or financial support pledged in the executive order to reunite these children with their families?

Let us be clear, Trump is significantly responsible for this. To begin with, he appointed Thomas Honan as acting head of ICE. Honan had long advocated for the separation of children from their families as a means of deterring illegal immigration. Honan and Trump confidante Stephen Miller were critical to instituting this program. Other Trump appointees, including Scott Lloyd, director of the Office of Refugee Resettlement, and Matthew Albence, from Immigration and Customs Enforcement, were also involved. This was part of Trump's "zero tolerance" policy.

The separations began as early as the summer of 2017 and went on for over a year. They were openly discussed within the administration. Trump knew what was happening, and for a long time did nothing.

The separations continued even as many observers reported horrendous conditions—poor hygiene, nutrition, and medical care, severe overcrowding, and absence of supervision. Everything about the children's care was bare bones and neglectful. Notably, some eyewitnesses reported seeing children in cages. As one example, Democrat senator Jeff Merkley described children "in wire-mesh, chain linked cages that are about 30x30 [feet], a lot of young folks put into them."

Yet, Trump allowed this to proceed until national and international opprobrium—including the Pope—reached fever pitch. That is, Trump did not end the program out of concern for children. He only bowed, in his own self-interest, to extreme and ever-accelerating pressure.

Then, as noted, Trump made no effort to ensure these families would be reunited.

Did we actually separate children from their mothers?

In Donald Trump's America, "Yes we did."

———————

May 18, 2019
The Mueller Report: Bungled Collusion Is Still Collusion
Dear Editors,

The Mueller Report was released about a month ago, giving us time for careful reading and reflection. The first part evaluated Russian interference in the 2016 election and the possible involvement of President Trump and/or his allies. The second part dealt with President Trump's alleged obstruction of the investigation.

One point is indisputable: The Russians interfered in the 2016 election.

As one example, we all know that Russia hacked Hillary Clinton's emails and released them, for Trump's benefit, and that Trump publicly encouraged that. As another, twelve Russian military officials were indicted for their interference. The Mueller Report details all sorts of Russian meddling.

That really was not in dispute. The real question for Robert Mueller and co-investigators was whether President Trump colluded with the Russians in their interference. Mueller found no evidence of that—no meetings, no phone calls, emails, or any kind of direct communication. Trump was legally absolved.

But, not so fast. Perhaps the most interesting part of the Russian interference story was the June 9 meeting at Trump Tower between a Russian attorney and Donald Trump Jr., Jared Kushner, and Paul Manafort. The meeting had been set up in an email to Trump Jr. promising "official documents and information that would incriminate Hillary and her dealings with Russia and would be very useful to [Trump Jr.'s] father," to which Trump Jr. responded, "I love it." And then he followed up.

Conservative Republican journalist Charles Krauthammer described that, paraphrasing, as de facto collusion. What else could you possibly call a meeting with a Russian operative explicitly to obtain derogatory information about your political opponent? Nothing came of the attempt, but Krauthammer also noted that "bungled collusion is still collusion." Hard to argue with that.

Then why didn't Mueller prosecute Trump Jr., Kushner, or Manafort for this overt collusion? Because of legal technicalities. Mueller felt that he could not meet "the government's burden to prove beyond a reasonable doubt that these individuals acted 'willfully' i.e., with 'general knowledge of the illegality of their conduct.'" That is to say, Mueller let them off mostly on the basis of their presumed ignorance, not absence of collusion. Simply that he could not prove that they knew they were breaking the law, not that they did not do what they obviously did.

As for President Trump, Mueller found no direct evidence that he knew of the June 9 meeting, though certainly no one involved was going to incriminate him. However, common sense—even if that is not legal evidence—dictates that Trump surely had to know and approve. Not only was this meeting a potential game-changer (would Don Jr. really keep a potential game-changer meeting from his father?), but the June 9 meeting was discussed ahead of time at a regular morning meeting of senior campaign staff, including Hope Hicks and Eric Trump. That is, most everyone knew! This was no secret. Donald Trump would have been about the only one not to know, and how could that be? But that could not be proven by legal standards, and Trump could also have pleaded "ignorance" of the law, just like the others.

Importantly, there is no contradiction between Krauthammer's common-sense view that multiple members of Trump's higher echelon, likely with Trump's approval, colluded with a Russian for the purpose of aiding Trump, and Mueller's conclusion that due to legal technicalities/requirements he could not bring charges. Both of them appear to have been correct judgments.

As for Part Two, Trump's alleged obstruction of the investigation: Mueller listed 10 instances in which Trump plausibly committed that crime and explicitly stated that he did not exonerate Trump. Instead, he made no judgment because as a sitting president, Trump was not subject to prosecution. However, Mueller clearly suggested that there was enough evidence—10 instances—of possible Trump obstruction that "[…] Congress may apply the obstruction laws to the President's corrupt exercise of the powers of office […]," presumably meaning potential impeachment. Mueller also stated that post-presidency the legal system would be justified in considering indictment. That meets both legal requirements and the "common sense standard."

To make the point in another way, over one thousand former federal prosecutors wrote that had Trump not been president, he would likely have been indicted for multiple charges of obstruction of justice.

The reality is that Mueller found a whole lot of incriminating evidence against Trump and his staff, and their best defense was legal technicalities. That is the law of the land, as applied to all of us, and entirely appropriate. But inability to prosecute is not the same as innocence, and certainly not the same as "moral innocence."

In this case, lay wisdom says for sure "yes" about Russian interference, "yes" about the June 9 meeting as collusion, "very likely" about Trump's knowledge and approval of that meeting, and "likely" about Trump committing multiple felony acts of obstruction of justice. He has not been indicted at this time, but legal and political jeopardy for Trump is still possible.

———————

December 1, 2019
The Impeachment Was Not a Farce
Dear Editors,

In Kevin Dowd's "impeachment is a farce" argument in the *New York Times*, he does not address the actual charge against President Trump—namely, that Trump withheld congressionally approved foreign aid for the purpose of pursuing personal favors. In fact, Dowd does not even mention the allegation, which was firmly established by Trump's own transcript, as well as the confirming comments of colleagues Rudy Giuliani and Mick Mulvaney, and a slew of apolitical career diplomats. Instead, Mr. Dowd can only resort to a series of irrelevancies and distortions, that "Ukraine didn't do the investigation and the aid was released [...] all aid is quid pro quo." Then he descended into name-calling: "obsessive zeal [...] Inspector Clouseau." The inability to confront the actual charge is disingenuous and an implicit acknowledgment that this impeachment is the opposite of farce.

Kevin, the allegation is that the aid was withheld, not that it wasn't ever released. The eventual release (after the gig was up) is irrelevant to the actual charge.

Similarly, the allegation is that Ukraine was asked to announce the investigation, not that they actually did it. Whether they did it or not is irrelevant to whether the request was made (and to why it was made).

Importantly, Republican Trump appointee Ambassador Sondland specifically noted that Ukraine was only asked to announce the investigation (to provide Trump a reelection talking point), and not to actually do it. In no way does this exonerate a president who asked for a return of purely personal interest, but without any national interest. All *quid pro quos* are not the same, and the ones that are OK do not exonerate the ones that are not OK. In that regard, it is notable that Republican Trump appointee John Bolton reportedly said, and did not deny, that Trump's foreign policy toward Turkey was guided by financial self-interest. Thus, Trump's Ukraine personal interest-based foreign policy may actually be business as usual for him.

When someone comes forth to criticize the impeachment as best he can, and this is all he has, it should make us even more confident of the impeachment's validity.

———————

September 4, 2020
Trump and John McCain: Draft Dodgers Should Keep Their Mouths Shut
Dear Editors,

President Donald Trump recently called fallen American soldiers "losers" and "suckers" and directed his staff to exclude disabled veterans from military parades.

That echoed his previous disparagement of the war hero, Senator John McCain, of whom Trump said, "He's not a war hero, he was a war hero because he was captured. I like people who weren't captured."

Both statements were, in statistical parlance, many standard deviations beyond normal human behavior, but if you can imagine this [...] it gets worse.

Based on overwhelming circumstantial evidence, all pointing in the same direction, Donald Trump is almost certainly a draft dodger. First, he received four student deferments from 1964 to 1968. When those were no longer attainable, he suddenly claimed bone spurs. Prior to that, he had played high-school baseball (superbly per his own telling) and was never hindered by bone spurs. After that, for the next 52 years, he never had bone spurs. The podiatrist who "diagnosed" them, Larry Braunstein, never publicly provided any substantiation over the next 39 years prior to his death in 2007. But his daughter, Elysa Braunstein, did speak up, saying that her dad, who rented his office from Fred Trump, fabricated the diagnosis "as a favor to Fred Trump" and that "It was family lore [...] something we would always discuss."

Acute bone spurs resolve, and would not be disqualifying for military service. Disqualification requires chronic discomfort and limitations, for which Trump has provided zero evidence ever since.

I actually do not castigate Trump for draft-dodging, especially not 52 years later. Vietnam was a horrible war, and Trump was among a cast of tens of thousands who dodged it.

However, the "Handbook for Dodging the Draft," and just a shred of common sense, says that if you successfully dodge the draft, keep your mouth shut forever, and certainly do not ever even think about criticizing someone who enlisted, served, and fought honorably. The latter is beyond the outer limits of decency!

———————

October 1, 2020
Is Not Paying Taxes "Smart?"
Dear Editors,

The *New York Times* recently obtained and reported on two decades of Donald Trump's tax returns. Notably, "Most of Mr. Trump's marquis enterprises—from his constellation of golf courses, to his conservative-magnet hotel in Washington—report losing millions, if not tens of millions, of dollars year after year." As a result, Trump paid no income taxes at all in 10 of the previous 15 years. Our erstwhile billionaire president paid almost no taxes!

With the election looming, what is there to learn from this?

We now know why Trump fought tooth-and-nail for years to prevent disclosure of his returns. To be clear, he did not commit tax fraud, but the returns paint a picture exactly the opposite of Trump's basic life story that he is so proud of—that of a fabulously successful businessman brilliantly accumulating vast wealth.

Actually, nobody should believe that Trump's core enterprises are losing money and failing year after year. These are just paper failures for the purposes of avoiding paying taxes. Several years ago, Trump stated that not paying taxes "makes me smart." By that he meant that he and his lawyers were smart enough to find sufficient loopholes, strategies, and bookkeeping ploys, whatever, to avoid paying taxes, thereby making successful businesses look unsuccessful on paper.

Trump is obviously not bothered by the elitist nature of "smart" in this context. The usual working person cannot use the loopholes and deductions available to the very wealthy. Furthermore, only the wealthy can afford the high-priced professional to find, exploit, and then defend these mechanisms. The rest of us cannot do that. We pay what we owe, or we get into trouble.

In the bigger picture, Trump's definition of "smart" means that very wealthy people in our system can find ways to pay less taxes and the government will have less money available for, as a few examples, national defense, debt reduction, and/or programs to help those in need. In Trump's case, the government suffered an enormous loss of funds that could have been used for these purposes.

Not paying taxes is effective for padding Trump's huge personal wealth, but is that a system that he endorses? Is that the message he wants to send to the rest of us? Be smart and hide your income? His perspective seems rather self-centered and detrimental to the greater good.

From a national perspective, Trump's "smart" seems stupid.

CHAPTER 2

TRUMP BOTCHES THE COVID-19 PANDEMIC

May 18, 2020
Hydroxychloroquine: A Medicine That Does Not Work for a Disease He Does Not Have
Dear Editors,

President Trump just announced that he has been taking hydroxychloroquine for over a week.

Hydroxychloroquine (HCQ) was given to patients infected with COVID-19 in the early stages of the pandemic. This was really a Hail Mary based on very preliminary evidence, but people were dying and we did not have anything of known value to offer. Nothing wrong with that.

However, as more data became available, it is now believed that HCQ is very likely ineffective in treating COVID-19 and is associated with cardiac arrhythmias that may even increase the incidence of death.

That is only the minor problem with Trump taking HCQ.

The bigger problem is that he does not have COVID-19! Thus, he is engaging in what might be called performative medicine, just for effect. His physician, Sean Coney, should probably be sanctioned by medical authorities for violating his Hippocratic oath. Prescribing a medicine to a patient to treat a disease he does not have cannot provide any benefit but exposes the patient to risks of side effects, in this case, the arrhythmias. That is taboo for physicians. Given how this probably took place, Trump demanding the treatment, "or else," it might be called "practicing medicine by fear of the patient."

This gets even worse.

The lede of this story is that the whole thing is calculated. Trump is making a point to the national audience. He is telling everyone, buttressing his message all along, not to worry about COVID-19 infection and not to follow expert advice on how to avoid it, because if you happen to get infected we have this great, highly effective, no side effects, medicine that will fix you in a jiffy. Look at me! I am taking it! COVID-19 is not a real thing. That was the point of his performance.

To sum that up, Trump is taking a medicine that does not work for a disease he does not have to make a false and dangerous point.

"What, me worry?" is a bizarre message to give when 88,000 people have died from COVID-19 in the United States, with no end in sight, and we still do not have any effective medicine to treat it.

I shudder to think how many people will needlessly die if they listen to Trump.

———————

May 11, 2023
Trump's Fear of Masks and the Lesson From Dialysis[1]
Dear Editors,

Donald Trump stated early in the COVID-19 pandemic that he would not wear a mask in order to prevent infection. He did not follow expert advice or

---

1 I learned about masks for COVID-19 early on through a good friend and very smart person, Dr. M.O., who led the COVID-19 task force at a major nearby university. He and his colleagues had the foresight to purchase N-95 masks for his hospital before the pandemic hit Chicago. The rest of us, early on, had only cheap, sometimes home-made, masks, and often had to re-use them. Out of kindness, Dr. M.O. offered to provide me with the quality masks purchased for his own hospital employees. I turned him down but the point was obvious: masks were important! I started wearing two of the lesser quality masks at all times, and even later on, when I gained access to better masks, I remained double-masked.

I also learned, from publicly available data, that over the first six months of the pandemic the infection rate was significantly higher in states that voted for Trump, and more commonly followed his mask-denying stance, than in those states that had voted for Clinton. And this was despite COVID-19's early geographical preference for population-dense east coast blue states, versus the lower population density of rural, typically red states.

Eventually, I had an eye-opening professional experience which clinched the value of masks, as discussed in this letter.

evidence. Instead, he said that masks make him look ridiculous and "sent the wrong message." In other words, a matter of vanity merging with politics. He repeatedly poked fun at Joe Biden for wearing a mask. His preoccupation with his image, and his indifference to others, ended up affecting other people in profoundly harmful fashion.

A number of observational epidemiological studies demonstrated the positive effect of masking. However, these studies were limited because out in the community, many important variables that influenced the results persisted—for example, length of exposure, distance, use and quality of masks, downtime of masking, and extent of disease detection.

Thus, I will share my own extensive professional experience as a kidney doctor treating many patients with dialysis, as it was a fortuitous experiment of nature in which all the major variables, mostly by happenstance, were essentially eliminated, and masks were put to a direct test.

Patients with end-stage renal disease requiring dialysis are treated in outpatient centers three times a week, each time for roughly four hours, typically flanked by two other patients 4–6 feet away. During the pandemic, dialysis providers gave every patient a new surgical mask with every treatment, and mask use was rigorously enforced by dialysis personnel. The compliance rate was virtually 100 percent! The patients were in a high-risk situation—indoors, with prolonged exposure to sometimes infected neighbors in their latent, asymptomatic, but never-the-less infectious periods. Masks were the only means to prevent infection transmission from patient to patient or patient to staff.

Further, since patients came to treatments three times a week and were evaluated by health care personnel every time, the detection of COVID-19 infections was optimal.

Patient-to-patient (or staff) transmission would be evident by a patient becoming ill and getting diagnosed, and then a neighboring patient getting ill several days later.

How well did the masks work?

In the several years of the pandemic, hundreds of my dialysis patients were diagnosed with COVID-19 infection. Remarkably, not a single transmission of infection from one patient to an adjacent patient or to staff was documented. This can only be attributed to the effectiveness of universal, proper masking.

Since this result was so dramatic, I posed the question to an international kidney chat room of almost 20,000 nephrologists: "Do you know of any dialysis patient diagnosed with COVID-19 a short time after being exposed to an infected neighboring patient?" Not a single nephrologist answered "yes!" There may have been some unrecognized transmissions, but this huge experience/natural experiment is compelling evidence for the effectiveness of enforced masking.

It also suggests that if and when the next airborne-transmitted viral pandemic strikes, the public health question we ask should not be "Do masks work?" but instead, "How do we provide everyone with easy access to good masks and convince everyone to wear them as directed?"

And, hopefully by then, we'll have a president not preoccupied with his personal appearance or political power to lead our national response.

———————

August 1, 2023
Trump's Nightmarish Response to COVID-19
Dear Editors,

Paul Krugman (*New York Times* op-ed writer) summarized the "national nightmare" of Trump's last year in office. Actually, I think he understated the insanity of Trump's response to the COVID-19 crisis. The latter is characterized by the following low points, in chronological sequence:

First, early on, with experts predicting a global calamity, Trump refused to make any preparations, for example, to stockpile personal protective equipment or ventilators, and routinely denied the problem with overtly false public statements like "we have it totally under control" and "one day, like a miracle, it will disappear." At a February 26 briefing he said, "We have fifteen people (with COVID-19), and the fifteen within a couple of days is going to be down to close to zero."

He kept derisively repeating the obnoxious phrase "the China Virus," which served no purpose other than to suggest that "this occurred on my watch, but it's not my fault, blame the Chinese."

Then, as bodies piled up here, including in refrigerated trucks outside of hospitals, he advised against and ridiculed any attempts to limit the spread of disease, including masks and distancing.

As the virus spread, he responded by saying that we were testing for COVID-19 too much, that testing "creates cases [...] makes us look bad," so we should "slow the testing down, please."

He championed failed and bogus treatments like hydroxychloroquine, ivermectin, and even suggested that injected household bleach could be useful. The claim of effective treatments was meant to assuage the public, uncomfortably reminiscent of Mad Magazine's spokesperson, Alfred E. Neuman, whose mantra was "What, me worry?"

As the election neared, he devolved into the delusional "COVID is a democrat hoax" and "nobody will be talking about COVID as soon as the election is over."

Actually, after the election, people kept dying and everyone kept talking about COVID-19 except [...] Donald J. Trump. Most tellingly, whereas he had long vociferously lauded the vaccine as "one of the greatest achievements of mankind [...] the Trump vaccine," and publicly demanded that it be approved before the election, once the election was over [...] utter silence. Trump rarely mentioned the vaccine again, and never actually advocated for anyone to take it. The abrupt silence suggested that his only motivation was using the vaccine to enable his reelection, and he had no interest in whether anyone actually benefited from it or if it saved lives.

One of the worst parts of Trump and COVID-19 is that he fueled a MAGA anti-science, anti-expert backlash, with his incessant criticism of the experts and their "fake science." That, and his eventual vaccine silence, contributed to many MAGAs refusing the vaccine. And dying.

There is much about COVID-19 to debate, but the irrationality of Trump's responses, one after the other after the other, is not really one of those things.

—————————

September 1, 2023
Did Trump Get Anything Right During COVID-19?
Dear Editors,

In response to the many justified criticisms of President Trump's management of the COVID-19 pandemic, we should also ask, "Did he get anything right?" And the answer is, of course he did, although Trump being Trump, even his good efforts come with qualifications.

The first good thing that he did, after several months of denial and not preparing, was to shut the country down and keep it that way for about two months, certainly limiting the death count. Though, actually, he was a bit slow—the National Basketball Association ended their season before Trump acted nationally—and he mostly just went with the flow, as nearly every affected country in the world did essentially the same thing. More than 3.9 billion people in more than 90 countries were asked or ordered to stay at home.

Even more to his credit, he sponsored Operation Warp Speed for vaccine development. Though, this too, was late. The COVID-19 virus sequence was announced on January 10 and vaccine work began about a week after that. Operation Warp Speed was not announced until four months later, on May 15. A bit slow and with questionable motives. Trump stopped talking about the vaccine and certainly did not advocate for it once the election was over. That suggested his motivation was self-interested—getting it approved fast in order to take credit and enable his reelection—without any real concern for whether anyone actually took the vaccine and benefited.

Furthermore, Trump undermined his own achievement with his steady downplaying of the virus—nothing really to worry about, a mixed message, to say the least—as well as his refusal to endorse the vaccine after the election. That led many people to shun the vaccine, and many of them died as a result.

Still, he put a lot of money into and emphasis on vaccine development and, regardless of his motivation, the vaccine saved a lot of people. Give him credit for that.

———————

February 2, 2024
The Defense of Trump Is Damning (to Him)
Dear Editors,

Roger Bate's dogmatic diatribe in the *New York Times* against "[...] all the bad ideas from COVID-19" attempts to defend Donald Trump from the harsh allegations against him.

However, Bate's essay contains several obvious large errors, the sort of flailing that invariably comes along with these attempts.

First, he calls (without explanation) the benefits of the COVID-19 vaccine "limited," which is contrary to all the data that showed it significantly reduced severe illness, hospitalization, and death.

Second, he criticizes the World Health Organization for prematurely declaring hydroxychloroquine and ivermectin as ineffective, implying that they turned out to be effective, when, in fact, they actually were proven ineffective. They are not considered plausible treatments for COVID-19.

Third, he calls the initial Swedish lax response to COVID-19 "remarkably effective" by comparing the Swedish COVID-19 death rate favorably to the United States. In lay terms, this is called comparing apples and oranges. Specifically, the United States has a significantly higher prevalence of obesity, diabetes, asthma, heart disease, and kidney disease, a higher population density and nursing home population, more people without medical insurance, and/or other reasons to have limited access to good medical care, all of which increase infection and death rates. A comparison of death rates in the United States with those in Sweden without considering these critical variables is uninterpretable and not considered an accepted scientific approach. Since this is well-known in academic circles, such a comparison should be considered intellectually dishonest.

On the other hand, unbiased people in the field did look at Swedish COVID-19 (and all-cause) death rates as compared with its three similar Scandinavian neighbors—Denmark, Norway, and Finland. The major difference among these countries with respect to COVID-19 was their responses. In contrast to Sweden, the neighboring countries opted for the more comprehensive and restrictive international approach. Unfortunately, the initial Swedish results were abysmal: Over the first year-plus, Sweden had a 4-10X (at some points, even greater) higher COVID-19 death rate than its three neighbors!

The King of Sweden and the Prime Minister spoke up about this in harsh terms, and the policymakers took note and reversed the lax Swedish approach to approximate typical U.S. strategies. When Sweden converted to more standard COVID-19 strategies, not surprisingly, the excess death rate of the previous lax approach significantly decreased over time.

Trump's COVID-19 management mirrored, in many ways, the initial lax Swedish approach—the one Sweden abandoned due to the many excess deaths.

If this is the best defense of Trump's COVID-19 policies, it is damning to him.

———————

June 8, 2024
The Trump-led Crusade Against Fauci: What Does It Say About Us?
(Published in the *Chicago Tribune*)
Dear Editors,

With regard to President Donald Trump and those in Congress criticizing Dr. Anthony Fauci's guidance in the COVID-19 pandemic: It's critically important to remember the conditions early on at the time decisions had to be made.

As a physician who worked in several Chicago-area hospitals throughout the pandemic, I can attest to that: These hospitals were filled to the brim with COVID-19 patients. Any additional patients would have been left in the halls or in the emergency room, waiting for a bed, nearly uncared for. Thus, plans were made for a convention center to be turned into a makeshift hospital—or, really, a way station to the morgue. There were so many COVID-19 patients who were so sick that physicians could barely tell them apart.

We ran out of critical supplies; for example, dialysis had to be rationed. Hospital personnel were stressed to the breaking point; in some hospitals, physicians such as nephrologists covered in the intensive care unit, where they were wholly untrained for the task. Hospitals in some areas kept refrigerated trucks outside to hold bodies.

Allowing COVID-19 to spread unchecked throughout the community would have led to large numbers of infected people without effective treatment available and even without hospital rooms. And alarmingly, no one knew when or even if the virus would ebb, or when or even if there would ever be a vaccine or effective treatment. For all we knew at the time, there was no end in sight; perhaps, even a Black Death-like toll loomed.

(If you think that is an exaggeration, you were not working in a hospital.)

That was the context in which decisions were made about masks, distancing, schools, lockdowns and the like. Not surprisingly, pretty much every country in the world acted in the same way, trying to prevent huge numbers of deaths.

Sweden, an exception, was more lax and suffered four to 10 times the COVID-19 death rate of its fellow Scandinavian countries in the first year. Sweden then changed course.

But only in the United States do we have congressional hearings in which some lawmakers, with the president's backing, call for the jailing of our most respected health care providers who did the best they could with limited information in hellacious circumstances and came to the same conclusions as other experts around the world.

Fauci estimated that COVID-19 precautions saved one million lives here.[2]

In the absence of political self-interest and/or self-aggrandizement, we thank those who helped save those lives.

———————

July 13, 2025
Republicans Raging Against Trump and His Vaccine. Who'd Have Thought?
Dear Editors,

Today, after a long hiatus, the COVID-19 vaccine returned to the news. Attorney General Pam Bondi dropped charges against a Utah doctor Michael

2 It is impossible to know if Fauci and his colleagues saved one million lives; that is merely an estimate. It is also impossible to know exactly how many deaths Trump's actions contributed to. But we do know that Fauci saved lives and Trump contributed to deaths. Which means that the congressional pursuit of Fauci, while giving Trump a free pass at the same time, inverts reality on its head.

Moore and three associates who had been indicted by a federal jury for allegedly discarding more than $28,000 worth of government-provided COVID-19 vaccines and distributing 1,937 fake COVID-19 vaccination cards in exchange for cash or required donations. Seemed like a pretty strong case, but that was before politics intervened and overrode justice. This is the same Bondi who fired a score of federal prosecutors, along with mere support staff, for doing their assigned jobs investigating Jan. 6 and other alleged crimes.

Bondi credited Rep. Marjorie Taylor Greene for prompting this. Greene called Dr. Moore "a hero who refused to inject his patients with a government mandated UNSAFE (emphasis mine) vaccine!"

RFK Jr. had previously said that Dr. Moore "deserved a medal for courage."

Bondi, Greene, and RFK Jr. seem to have forgotten that this is the self-named "Trump Vaccine." During his first term, nobody touted this vaccine or tried to accelerate its development more than Trump, the appropriately proud father of Operation Warp Speed. He sometimes described it as his greatest accomplishment.

While pursuing the far-right wing agenda of opposing science, vaccines, and evidence, they are damning President Trump. It is his vaccine that Greene said is unsafe, allegedly having caused harm to so many unsuspecting Americans.

September 8, 2025
The COVID-19 Vaccine Mandate and Personal Freedom
Dear Editors,

The COVID-19 vaccine and its previous mandates recently returned to public attention, relating both to RFK Jr.'s congressional hearing and to Florida's decision to eliminate mandatory childhood vaccines.

That decision was based on the view that mandates are unacceptable, that we all get to decide what we put, or do not put, into our bodies, and the government should have no say in the matter.

President Trump put fuel on that fire years ago when he opposed mandates for his administration's COVID-19 vaccine.

Subsequently, President Biden, along with numerous states and municipalities, enacted vaccine mandates, but they have been generally misunderstood, and the misunderstanding, unfortunately, fed more anti-vaccine backlash and led to many unnecessary deaths.

The COVID-19 vaccine mandates never stated that anyone had to take the vaccine. No one was arrested for refusing. Anyone could choose not to take the vaccine, in which case, one was simply not allowed to enter certain areas, mostly health care facilities, workplaces, schools, stores, arenas, and the like, because, if infected with COVID-19, one could infect many others. The vaccine mandates were simply requirements for certain situations, but not forced upon anyone. Even then, many private employers allowed workers who refused the vaccine to continue to work if they wore masks and submitted to regular testing. It may not have been a choice they liked, but employees had a choice.

The requirement for a vaccine in certain areas was not meant to be punitive or to intrude upon personal freedom, or even primarily to protect the vaccinated individual from illness. At a time the virus was prevalent, highly infectious, and potentially lethal, and with no effective treatment available, the COVID-19 vaccine mandate was intended to prevent infected patients from transmitting disease to others. And in some enclosed workplaces and gathering areas, to prevent events of large-scale transmission.

This is consistent with the long-standing principle delineating the limits of personal freedom. Supreme Court justice Oliver Wendell Holmes Jr. famously said, "The right to swing my fist ends where the other man's nose begins." Or, my freedom ends at the tip of your nose. Personal freedom is not, contrary to what anti-vaxxers suggest, immune to regulation. Many laws restrict our behavior, the interests of public health being just one example.

Similarly, laws also require you to do things in the interests of other people, for example, to obtain a license so that you may drive or perform many jobs, to pay taxes, to report if drafted by the military, even to keep your front lawn mown. These laws advanced us from lawless chaos, in which everyone did whatever they wanted, to a civilized society, in which we give up some freedoms in the interests of the collective good.

People who chose not to get vaccinated died at a much higher rate than those who opted for the vaccine. That was their choice, and it was respected by the law. At the same time, mandates served their purpose: At a time COVID-19 was most prevalent and injurious, the mandates reduced the transmission of the often lethal virus from one person to others, saving lives in the process. That was clearly in the interests of public health. When COVID-19 eventually became less prevalent and less virulent, the vaccine requirements were lifted.

Both groups of people, pro- and anti-vaxxers, had their decisions respected. It was the consequences of those decisions that differed.

CHAPTER 3

THE JAN. 6 INSURRECTION

March 1, 2020
Jan. 6: A Hairbreadth's Escape for All of Us
Dear Editors,

House Speaker Kevin McCarthy recently traveled to President Trump's Mar-A-Lago home, apparently to ask forgiveness from Trump for the crime Trump committed. Hopefully, this is not a harbinger for the rest of the Republican Party eventually capitulating as well.

Two points come to mind about January 6th.

First, it is hard to imagine a worse non-homicidal crime than what Trump attempted, trying to insert himself as a non-elected president of the United States. It is not a stretch to say he tried to overthrow the government. Joe Biden was elected president; Trump tried to prevent him from taking office so that he could do so instead. This was a crime against a basic tenet of democracy: that we have elections, they are sacrosanct, the winner takes office, not the loser. Had Trump succeeded, the basis of our country's founding and our entire way of life would have gone up in smoke. An unelected person, simply by dint of his own force, intimidation, and power, would have replaced the elected president.

This was a crime against all Americans. It is hard to overstate the perfidy here.

Second, we should not forget how close Trump came to succeeding. Ultimately, one man, Vice President Mike Pence, stood in his way, and only after outside consultation. Pence couldn't figure this out by himself. He called retired Republican federal judge J. Michael Luttig and Republican ex-vice president Dan Quayle for advice. Both told Pence that the Constitution demanded that he certify Biden's election victory. Pence still hesitated, at least in his phone call with Quayle, before finally following their advice. For a scary period of time, whether or not he would abide by the Constitution was up in the air.

Further, we don't know exactly why Pence called Quayle and Luttig rather than other Republicans, but there probably was some randomness involved. What if Quayle and Luttig were unavailable? What if Pence called two other Republican confidantes? There certainly were plenty of alternatives around, at least some of whom would have given Pence the opposite advice, which he probably would have followed.

Thus, the favorable end result, the preservation of the republic, may simply have reflected who Pence happened to call, which is not a strong basis for democracy to stand on.

There was no precedent to what would have happened if Pence refused to certify. Nobody really knows; the outcome would have been uncertain, and a Trump presidency plausible. In fact, one sequela commonly discussed was that the election would have gone back to the House, where Republicans controlled more states, likely leading to a Trump victory.

Which means that not only did Trump attempt to overthrow the government, he came within a hair's breadth of succeeding.

————————

August 12, 2023
Jan. 6 Crime: The Defense Is Incriminating
Dear Editors,

Regarding David French's (*New York Times* op-ed writer) summary and analysis of likely arguments for and against Trump in the Jan. 6 and related events trial:

Prosecution:

1) "[…] you're describing what you want the law to be, not what it is […] the existing case law is on (our) side."
2) "Every single count is supported not just by the text but also by a vast amount of precedent."

3) "The indictment describes in detail Trump's intimate cooperation with his co-conspirators. Are you arguing that they were acting on their own?"
4) "First year law students learn [...] 'There is no First amendment privilege to commit crimes.'"

For the defense: hard to pick out anything that made much sense and wasn't fully rebutted.

French is a conservative writer and this was an attempt to put the best light on both sides. Particularly in that context, his essay was notable for how compelling it was for the prosecution. Perhaps inadvertently, he makes a telling point.

———————

August 16, 2023
Trump Versus Gore: Nothing Important in Common
Dear Editors,

Noted lawyer and commentator Alan Dershowitz recently described Donald Trump's post-election actions as very similar to Al Gore's after the 2000 presidential election. Republican presidential candidate Chris Christie disagreed, noting that after Gore's legal strategy failed, he conceded the election, whereas Trump continued to contest the election results with extrajudicial machinations (which are the basis of his indictments.)

Christie's distinction is critical, but he, too, mischaracterized the 2000 election, fostering popular myths. In reality, Gore's behavior differed from Trump's right from the start, not just after his legal strategy failed.

Myth: Al Gore demanded a recount in order to reverse the original Florida election results.

Fact: The recount was prompted automatically by Florida law based on the closeness of the count. Gore did not instigate the recount.

Myth: Al Gore appealed all the way to the U.S. Supreme Court.

Fact: George Bush appealed to the U.S. Supreme Court, contesting a ruling by the Florida Supreme Court. That is, BOTH Gore and Bush understandably appealed rulings averse to their own interests.

In summary, the Florida recount was mandated by law and the subsequent appellate process was perpetuated by both Gore and Bush. This was not a unilateral effort by Gore to overturn an election in the absence of any evidence to support that.

The elections of 2000 and 2020 both fall under the broad genre of "contested elections." Beyond that, they have nothing important in common.

——————————

November 6, 2024
We Didn't Really Need the Jan. 6 Commission
Dear Editors,

Donald Trump was just elected president and his federal prosecutions will end; he is getting away with probably the Crime of the Century. Voters knew this, they elected him anyway, that's how democracy works, and continues to work now that we survived Trump's attempt to end it by inserting himself into power as a non-elected president.

Why did so many MAGA voters put this crime to the side? For sure, many saw other attributes in Trump, which is their right, and the Democrats had some major flaws. But many voters also—and this is hard to believe—argued that the Jan. 6 events were hyperbolized, overrated, not something to hold against him. Let's consider some of those arguments.

First, that it wasn't an insurrection because there were no guns at the Capitol and an insurrection requires guns. That is false, irrelevant, and unimportant. Guns were confiscated at the Capitol, and we also know there were a huge number of guns at the preceding rally; Trump actually complained that the gun monitors at the entrances were minimizing his crowd size (there we go again, about crowd size). More importantly, the legal definition of insurrection does not require guns—under 18 U.S.C. § 2383, insurrection refers to any act of rising against the authority of the state or its laws. No mention at all of firearms or weapons of any kind.

Furthermore, the legal charge of insurrection has a difficult burden of proof, and Special Prosecutor Jack Smith properly chose his indictments conservatively, as both a technical and legal issue. But that is wholly different from how the public should think of the crime. Because, whether you call it an insurrection or not, Trump attempted to prevent an elected president from assuming office so that he, an unelected candidate, could do so instead. And to do so, he pressured his vice president to ignore his constitutional duty and sent an agitated mob to the Capitol in pursuit of his goal.

But, it is said, he told the protesters to "go peacefully." Yes, he did, but that must be put in context. Jan. 6 was the culmination of a two-month effort to overturn the election, including summoning people to the Capitol who never would have been there otherwise, and telling them over and over again, "Be strong [...] take your country back [...]." The single "go peacefully" comment was last minute, completely at odds with everything else, and after the mob was already riled up. In context, that came across like a mob chieftain advising his thugs to take care of someone or something, but to do so peacefully, wink wink. That is, a last second superficial ploy to eventually help yourself in court. Nobody should be fooled.

Trump also sat quietly in the White House while the Capitol was breached. If he was serious about "go peacefully," he would have immediately screamed, "No, Stop, That's Not What I Meant." Obviously, he liked what he saw, as it was a means to "take your country back"; that is, stop the certification.

It is also claimed by some that Trump had no "intent," that he did not know the mob would storm the Capitol. Likely, there is some truth to that; perhaps Trump did not have the specifics in mind, only the general idea that somehow the mob had to stop the certification of the election so that eventually he could claim power. But when the boss tells his thugs to get something done, even without specific details, the mobster is responsible for how the thugs get that thing done. In addition, sending an angered mob to the Capitol was reckless, like speeding or drunk driving or tossing a baseball out of a 40th floor window, and we are responsible under the law for the sequelae of reckless actions.

It is claimed that the Jan. 6 Commission was a sham, "all Democrats." Well, almost all Democrats except Liz Cheney and Adam Kinzinger, but, so what? The important thing was not the composition of the Committee, but the actual testimony, and that was virtually all by Republicans, many of them appointed by or once working for Trump—hard to call them biased. Furthermore, virtually all the testimony went unrebutted, except by name-calling. Trump claimed that was the Committee's fault; they didn't call people who would defend him to testify, but the reality is that no one of that ilk ever surfaced. There is not a single example of someone publicly saying, "I want to testify, I have exonerating information, but the Committee won't allow me." Actually, it was the opposite: Trump supporters under oath sometimes took the 5th Amendment—refusing to testify. And five House Republicans (Jim Jordan, Kevin McCarthy, Scott Perry, Mo Brooks, and Andy Biggs) refused to comply with subpoenas demanding their testimony.

To this day, the voluminous testimony by more than one hundred Republicans remains unrebutted.

Of course, we did not really need the Jan. 6 Commission, as everything important happened in plain sight. In his unrelenting quest to be an unelected president, Trump summoned supporters to Washington, stirred them up and sent them to the Capitol. When it turned violent, his silence egged them on. Democracy escaped, but only by a whisker, and only against the wishes of Donald Trump and his mob.

———————

November 28, 2024
Trump's Crime in Georgia
Dear Editors,

Three problems with Thomas Goldstein's "It's Time to Drop Criminal Cases Against Trump":

First, after he aptly writes "A central pillar of American democracy is that no man is above the law," he follows with, "But Mr. Trump isn't an ordinary man." Seems like the whole point of the dictum Goldstein cites is that there are no exceptions; that Mr. Trump, like Mr. Nixon before him, is in fact an ordinary man in the eyes of the law. The opposite guts the central pillar of American democracy that has governed our thinking for over 200 years.

Second, another central pillar of our republic that Mr. Goldstein upends is that alleged crimes ought to be judged by the legal system and not by popular vote. Related, Mr. Goldstein presumes, without evidence, unfair partisan rulings.

He then ignores the appeals process, which is in place to correct any unwarranted rulings.

And finally, Mr. Goldstein likens the Georgia case to the New York case against Trump as "unusual" and "political." Unlike the New York case, the Georgia case involves an alleged crime of major proportions: the attempted overthrow of a properly elected government in order to institute an unelected person as president. The alleged attempt to illegally change the results of the Georgia voting was an important part of that scheme and surely, if proven, represents a violation of Georgia electorate as well as Georgia law. It seems wrong to so blithely dismiss such a massive crime.

———————

January 6, 2025
Jan. 6 Anniversary: The Three Stooges
Dear Editors,

Today is the fifth-year anniversary of the Jan. 6 Crime of the Century and we now know that Donald Trump is going to get away with it. How is this even possible? As is almost always the case, there are multiple reasons, but I think three men were critically important as the Moe, Larry, and Curly surrogates. I refer to Mitch McConnell, Merrick Garland, and John Roberts.

Senator McConnell was properly aghast as Jan. 6 unfolded, saying "If this isn't impeachable, I don't know what is." And, "The Democrats are going to take care of the son of a bitch for us," meaning impeachment and conviction. The first part, by the House of Representatives, proceeded as expected. Conviction by the Senate would then have served two important purposes: First, justice, ensuring that Trump was punished for his crime. Second, preventing him from ever returning to office.

But after his initial ire, McConnell quickly changed course. He closed the Senate to make sure the vote would not take place until after Trump left office and then he stated that he was voting "no" because a president cannot be impeached when he is out of office (made up out of "emperor's clothes" and not contained in the U.S. Constitution). That is, he purposefully created a situation that would allow him to vote "no." That provided cover and impetus for other Senate Republicans to follow suit. As enough did, influenced by McConnell, Trump got off. McConnell's dishonesty recapitulated his previous shenanigans during the Obama and Trump Supreme Court nominations. Clearly, McConnell will easily compromise himself in his own perceived self-interests and those of his party.

Presumably, he decided that Trump's conviction in the Senate would damage Republican senators and the Republican Party. Better to leave the punishment to Attorney General Merrick Garland—it would still be a disgrace, but not on McConnell's watch, and not requiring Republican senators to face the MAGA base after a vote to convict. Much better for Trump's downfall to come at the hands of a Democrat attorney general and Biden's Department of Justice.

Unfortunately, Garland did not save McConnell. I hate to cast aspersions on Garland because he seems an honorable man, but he too simply failed to do his job, which is to oversee the prosecution of crime. It was obvious that this was the most significant crime he would ever see, so Garland should have immediately started an investigation and proceeded to trial in a reasonable time frame. But for unknown reasons, he let Congress investigate first, rather than do his own work. By the time Congress finished and a special prosecutor, Jack Smith, was appointed to conduct another investigation, and indictments were finally handed down—it had taken long enough to allow the third of the Three Stooges to finish off this multi-step exercise in subverting justice. Garland could not have known the Supreme Court would do what they did; he may have thought it inconceivable, but that was no excuse for dawdling, and his dawdling came back to haunt him.

The final member of the triad, the third Stooge, was none other than John Roberts, the chief justice of the Supreme Court. To be fair, he is just one justice and the court as a whole purposely delayed ruling on Trump's suit. However, as chief justice, he had the sway, and even responsibility, to see that an alleged crime of this magnitude saw its day in court. He knew that undue delay would prevent the cases from being heard before the election, and that if Trump won the election, the cases would end. Regardless of how he felt personally, Roberts should have prevented that outcome; instead, he enabled it. This is on all the justices who went along with the delay, but mostly on Roberts, who was in charge. This happened on his watch. What did not happen on his watch was a trial and a verdict. Justice denied!

To sum up: McConnell did not do his job, Garland did not do his job, and Roberts did not do his job.

One, two, three; Moe, Larry, and Curly. Trump needed all three to go scot-free.

Sept 2, 2025
Trump and the Chutzpah of the Jan. 6 Rioters
Dear Editors,

A lawyer representing the pardoned Jan. 6 criminals recently asked the Justice Department to create a special panel for the purpose of providing them financial reparations for the damage they suffered at the hands of the federal government.

There is a word in Yiddish for this—chutzpah—meaning, extreme audacity. This request is audacious even for chutzpah; it is unparalleled, unimaginable chutzpah. There is not a word in any language that can capture the insanity of this request.

The Jan 6. criminals trespassed on and damaged an iconic federal building, threatened to hang Vice President Mike Pence, to assault the Speaker of the House, Nancy Pelosi, disrupted a government proceeding, injured police officers, and for many hours prevented Congress from certifying our elected president. Their goal was to prevent the legal transfer of power, one of our country's most fundamental, time-honored, and respected procedures. It makes us who we are. They did all this in broad daylight, on national television—hard to imagine less defensible crimes. As a result, many of them pled guilty, and the ones who insisted on their day in court lost 99 percent of the cases. Many of them received prison sentences of up to 22 years.

There was little public pushback to these sentences. How could there be? At trial, these defendants had so little to say on their own behalf that many of them resorted to "But I was only doing what President Trump told me to do."

Then, a series of miracles took place, at least for these convicted criminals. First, Trump escaped prosecution for orchestrating the insurrection. Then, he was reelected president. Then, for his own purposes, to perpetuate and further sanitize his Big Lie, his enduring delusion that he actually won the 2020 election, he pardoned all of them.

At that point, these convicted criminals should have thanked their lucky stars, over and over and over again, every day for the rest of their lives. When they were sentenced to prison, they could not have even imagined this fortunate outcome. But there they were, free to go. They should have gone quietly, just grateful to be out of jail.

That did not happen. Instead, we have a request for compensation, which is a thumb in our collective eyes. Now this is *chutzpah*! Any compensation money will come from our tax dollars, yours and mine. It would be a complete inversion of justice: the victims of a crime paying the criminals.

Trump, of course, is responsible for all of this. He created the Big Lie, summoned the rioters to Washington, directed them to the Capitol, urged them to "be strong" and "be wild" and to "take our country back." He sat by and watched the riot on TV, along with the rest of us. Then, he pardoned the criminals as soon as he could. None of this happens without him.

He can spare all of us yet another indignity with a common sense phone call to the Justice Department forbidding these proposed reparations. But if past predicts future, that is unlikely.

PART TWO

Campaigning for Reelection 2024

CHAPTER 4

THE CASE AGAINST TRUMP

July 31, 2024
Kenya, Nimbra, Now India: Xenophobia
Dear Editors,

Donald Trump recently made a very odd and telling comment about Kamala Harris:

> "I didn't know she was Black until a number of years ago when she happened to turn Black and now she wants to be known as Black. So, I don't know, is she Indian or is she Black?"

No one who has ever known Harris has ever questioned her racial identity, but, actually, that is not the point. The point is that Trump routinely picks on his opponents' foreign backgrounds as if they are valid criticisms, things to be ashamed of, things to cover up.

This recalled Trump's obsessive fixation on President Barack Obama's birthplace. Trump famously, and for years, falsely claimed that Obama was born in Kenya, thus giving his imprimatur to the so-called birther conspiracy. At one point, Trump claimed to have private investigators in Hawaii about to break the big news about Obama and his real place of birth. Obama's mother was American born so there was no question about Obama's citizenship or eligibility for the presidency; this was just, in Trump's bizarre worldview, an attempt to disparage Obama based on his nationality.

He also referred to ex-governor presidential candidate Nikki Haley, the daughter of Indian immigrants, as Nimbra, mocking her birth name, as if that somehow suggested that she was a lesser person.

First Kenya, then, Nimbra, now "is she Indian or is she Black?".

Why is Trump so preoccupied with nationality? Why does he think it is something to denigrate?

I believe the word for that is xenophobia, the dislike and fear of people from other places.

———————

August 24, 2024
The Litany of Trump's Felonies and Sins
Dear Editors,

The current conventional political wisdom is that Kamala Harris must provide more detail about her policies to enable her election.

But could this election be an exception to the rule? Consider the following:

Donald Trump's recent 34-count felony conviction for falsifying business records followed a lifetime of unlawful activity. Here are the specifics:

—He was found liable for sexual abuse.
—Then, for defamation of the woman he abused.
—His company was found guilty of tax fraud and falsifying business records.
—He withheld foreign aid for Ukraine in a quest for personal favors.
—He is under indictment for attempting to overthrow the government/election (Several of his co-conspirators have pleaded guilty and several of his lawyers have lost their licenses.)
—He is under indictment for illegally taking classified documents and then obstructing the investigation.
—He settled a case with a large financial penalty for refusing, with his father, to rent apartments to blacks and Hispanics.
—He was found liable for running a fraudulent university and fined $25 million.
—He admitted to running a fraudulent charity (a fraudulent charity!) and paid another large fine.
—He dodged the draft with bone spurs that were never documented or treated and that did not persist or ever recur.

—Under the category of nothing is too small to violate, Trump paid a $2,500 fine for violating tax laws by contributing to Pam Bondi's political action committee. (Ms. Bondi, then Florida's attorney general, refrained from joining the multi-state lawsuit against Trump University.)

—The remainder of the list of other old and/or pending lawsuits against him is too preposterously long for this letter.

True, Trump has to date evaded conviction and liability for some, but not all, of the above, owing variably to his and his father's influence, legal technicalities, and/or his own appointed friends in high places, including the courts. However, none of that changes the reality of the crimes and his sordid history.

Further, these crimes are tied together in several unifying and recurrent themes.

His fraudulent university, fraudulent charity, defaults on debts, deceptive use of campaign contributions from cash-strapped supporters to pay his legal bills, and more, all suggest that Trump is a con man, a high profile grifter without precedent.

His refusal to rent to blacks and Hispanics, his vitriolic comments about the Central Park Five, his Obama birther conspiracy fixation, his reference to Black Lives Matter as a "symbol of hate," his defense of Confederate statues and leaders, all suggest racism.

His references to Muslims as terrorists, to Latino immigrants as drug dealers and rapists, to "shithole countries" and "judges of Mexican heritage," all smack of xenophobia.

His sexual abuse and joyful comments about grabbing women's private parts and about women being ugly (Carly Fiorina and Ted Cruz's wife) or "bleeding from wherever" (Megyn Kelly) suggest misogyny.

Separate from actual crimes are his bizarre raves and rants, ranging from the trivial and absurd (crowd sizes, doctored pictures, Ted Cruz's dad and the JFK assassination, etc.) to the important and serious (the "Big Lie" about the 2020 election). Taken together, this repetitive behavior suggests a disordered thought process. His public ridicule of people with disabilities and medical illnesses, military heroes, and Gold Star parents, and much more, also falls outside the realm of normal mental functioning.

Alone among world leaders, he dismissed the seriousness of the COVID-19 pandemic.

Maybe most callous of all, after 9/11, he called into a television station to point out that his building was now the tallest in Manhattan.

As a result of all of that, scores of prominent conservative Republicans, including many whom he appointed to work closely with him, such as former chief of staff John Kelly, a previous Republican president and vice president, a previous Republican presidential nominee, and his historically obsequious vice president Mike Pence, no longer support him. That is unprecedented in American history.

Perhaps this is an election in which character, morality, empathy, and mental stability should be the compelling distinctions between the two candidates.

———————

September 12, 2024
Trump's Comically Insane Debate Performance
Dear Editors,

Included in the slew of comically insane comments Donald Trump made at the recent presidential debate:

—Immigrants are eating cats and dogs in Ohio.
—Democrats favored repealing *Roe v. Wade.*
—Joe Biden hates Kamala Harris.
—Harris only recently identified as Black.
—60 consecutive judges (including Republican and Trump-appointed) were prejudiced against him.
—He will end the Ukraine-Russia war in one day.
—He saved Obamacare.
—Democrats support execution of babies after birth.
—Transgender operations are done in schools during school days.

In the aftermath of what was widely regarded as a debacle for him, Trump said that:

—Harris had been fed the questions.
—He had a perfect debate.
—In a post-debate poll, around 90 percent of responders declared him the winner.

There is no rational explanation for that utter craziness.

——————————

September 13, 2024
Laura Loomer: You Can Tell a Lot About a Man by the Company He Keeps
Dear Editors,

Far-right-wing influencer and provocateur Laura Loomer traveled multiple times recently with President Trump on his private airplane. She clearly has direct access to him, and apparently, not only his ear, but his trust. He has praised her, shared her posts, and seems to value her opinions.

Loomer is clearly untethered and off-the-wall. For example, she has stated that 9/11 "was an inside job," fully espoused the Big Lie, and claimed that Kamala Harris is not black. She followed that with the racist comment "If Harris wins, the White House will smell like curry." She stated that Harris "wore a secret earpiece" at the presidential debate. She has a long history of anti-Muslim racism, including the comment that "Islam is a cancer of humanity." The wackiness goes on and on.

Trump hanging out with Laura Loomer recalls the old adage, "You can tell a lot about a man by the company he keeps."

——————————

September 23, 2024
Eating Cats and Dogs
(Published in the *Chicago Tribune*)
Dear Editors,

A recent CBS news poll found that two-thirds of Trump supporters believe Haitian immigrants in Ohio are kidnapping pets and eating them, similar to the percentage of Republicans who believe the 2020 election was stolen.

To say the obvious, both of these claims are without evidence and preposterous.

In the history of American politics up until now, malicious assertions like these would have been considered immediately disqualifying for a presidential candidate from either party.

Thus, they went from disqualifying to believed.

Future historians will address: How could that happen?

———————

September 28, 2024
Delusional or Pathological Liar?
Dear Editors,

In her co-written column "We Cannot Go On Like This," *New York Times* editorialist Gail Collins supported Kamala Harris on the basis that "[...] at least she's sane." She presumably was referring in part to Donald Trump's routine espousal of preposterous things, including, among others, that the 2020 election was stolen (despite 60+ consecutive judges ruling against him), and that immigrants are kidnapping and eating cats and dogs in Ohio. Either he believes these things to be true or he does not. If the former applies, he is delusional. If he is knowingly telling malicious and divisive lies, that suggests a personality disorder, with pathological lying as a component. Either way, as Ms. Collins writes, "sane" does not seem to apply.

———————

September 29, 2024
Trump's Psychopathology, From the Experts
Dear Editors,

In his 9/25 letter to the *New York Times*, retired psychiatrist Donald Mender called for the American Psychiatric Association to "assemble an independent task force, collectively charged with a frank and expeditious review of Donald Trump's known behavior." This was essentially done years ago, in the book "The Dangerous Case of Donald Trump" (2017, updated in 2019) co-authored by 37 eminent psychiatrists and mental health specialists. Among other things, these experts variably described Trump as a delusional sociopath having "psychological impairment [...] extreme hedonism," and a "major personality disorder." And that was before the unending Big Lie of the 2020 election, the recent claims that 60 consecutive judges were biased against him, that Haitians are kidnapping and eating pets in Ohio. Another update would surely be an even more scathing description of his psychiatric disorder.[1]

———————

October 2, 2024
Vance Better Than Trump!
Dear Editors,

Here is my main take-home point from the vice president debate: J. D. Vance continued to back Donald Trump's comically awful, malicious, preposterous assertions that the 2020 election was stolen and that Haitian immigrants are kidnapping and eating cats and dogs in Ohio. However, outside of that he tried to present himself as a normal, sane, mature adult, with empathy for others,

---

1 Many Republicans objected to *The Dangerous Case of Donald Trump* on the basis of the American Psychiatric Association's 1973 guideline, termed the "Goldwater Rule," which states that it is unethical for a psychiatrist to offer a professional opinion on the mental state of a public official unless they have personally examined that individual. Clearly, the psychiatrists who contributed to "The Dangerous Case of Donald Trump" violated that guideline.

Psychiatrists should, indeed, tread very carefully in these instances. But, with hindsight 50 years later, the Goldwater Rule should be reconsidered. First, it is obvious that you do not need to examine someone to make a general diagnosis of mental illness. For example, if you see someone walking naked down 5th Avenue in Manhattan screaming "I am Jesus," you wouldn't even need to be a psychiatrist to reach that conclusion. You would require a professional examination to make a precise psychiatric diagnosis, but that is besides the point. Based on cursory observation, the person is indisputably very ill. Second, it surely is in the public interest for a trained psychiatrist to share such an opinion of a presidential candidate with the public, especially if large numbers of psychiatrists agree. The alternative would be to keep mum—out of respect for a long-ago stated principle—and thereby risk the election of a psychiatrically damaged president. Why would we consider that a better option?

and with some tolerance of contrary opinions. That part distinguished him from Donald Trump.

———————

October 6, 2024
Trump From People Who Know Him: The Most Frightening Political Journalism Ever
(Published in the *New York Times*)
Dear Editors,

"The Trump Testimonials: The Case Against Him From His Own People" by the editorial board (October 6)—in which 91 of his "own people" described him variably as deranged, psychiatrically damaged, basically dangerous—was the most frightening political journalism I have ever read.

Never in the history of American politics have so many people in a candidate's inner orbit, in the know, largely in the same party, often Trump-appointed, spoken in such vitriolic, even apocalyptic terms about a presidential candidate.

And nearly all of their alarming comments preceded our learning that Donald Trump responded to the potential hanging of Mike Pence with "So what?"; his comically preposterous assertions that Haitians are kidnapping and eating cats and dogs in Ohio; his assertion that transgender operations are being done on schoolchildren during school hours; and his being found liable for sexual assault and guilty of falsifying business records.

Yet these dire warnings, from so many so close to Mr. Trump, fall upon deaf ears in roughly half the American populace.

It is the oddest thing I've seen in my 69 years.

———————

January 1, 2025
The 2024 Election: Would Lincoln Have Won?
Dear Editors,

Michelle Cottle's criticism ("The 2024 High School Yearbook of American Politics" *New York Times*) of Kamala Harris as the "Most Ill Prepared" seems unnecessarily harsh.

For sure, Harris seemed too scripted, had several mediocre interviews, and suffered from previous stances on issues that were hard to overcome, but no candidate is perfect, and she also did many good things. Broadly speaking, she presented an optimistic, respectful worldview that contrasted to Trump's often dishonest and sometimes apocalyptic rage. Specifically, she presented economic policies that most experts considered superior to Trump's plans. She also presented reasonable, if not innovative, plans for taxes, immigration, health care, and other issues. Importantly, based on both personality and policies, she dominated Trump in their debate so badly that he refused to debate again. And, 75 million Americans voted for her.

Furthermore, and in retrospect, it is not clear she ever had much of a chance, as most of Trump's voters seemed out of her reach from the start.

Two-thirds of Trump voters, or about fifty-five million, indicated in polls that they believed the Big Lie of the 2020 election. Roughly the same number believed the absurd Haitian pet-eating myth. Very likely, those respondents mostly overlap, but not 100 percent, so there may have been 60–65 million voters in a Trump cult world, willing to believe anything he said, no matter how ridiculous or absurd. Then, there were additional voters who simply would never vote for a woman, a black, or someone with Indian heritage. We cannot know how many but, of course, not zero, and then there are evangelical one-issue abortion voters and those seeking tax cuts for themselves.

Still not done: What about those many voters understandably worried about the high price of food, gas, rents, and so on? Why didn't they heed the advice of the 23 Nobel Prize winning economists (and other Wall Street and financial mavens) who stated that Harris's economic plan was "vastly superior" to Trump's? That stance seemed like more blind faith in Trump. That adds up to a whole lot of Trump voters simply out of reach from the start.

This is not meant to disparage those voters, but to point out that nothing Harris could have said or done would have won them over.

Add them all up: Abraham Lincoln might not have beaten Trump!

———————

January 6, 2025
Redefining Expertise: I Think I am an Expert, Therefore I Am
Dear Editors,

James Carville discussed ("Why I Was Wrong About the 2024 Election") the role of the economy and the failed Democrat messaging in fueling Donald Trump's victorious election.

However, he missed a key point. The voters who emphasized their financial straits obviously ought to have voted for the candidate with the better economic plan. Yet Trump's proposed tax cuts for the wealthy and heavy tariffs did not bode well for people in need.

Tellingly, in the vice presidential debate, when J. D. Vance was confronted with the analysis of 23 Nobel Prize winners who preferred Harris's economic plans over Trump's, and knowing that no Nobel Prize winners came to Trump's defense, all he could say was that he "did not believe the experts," and that Trump was the expert. Many voters, somehow, bought that lame expert-by-proclamation answer.

This echoes Trump, the notorious draft-dodger, saying that "I know more about war than my generals."[2]

Traditionally, experts are recognized within a field and are respected for their education, knowledge, training, and experience. Trump and Vance show no respect for authentic, earned expertise. Their view is that you can simply claim it for yourself.

---

2 Later in the year, contradicting widely accepted medical wisdom, Trump urged pregnant women not to take Tylenol. He endorsed an unproven link of Tylenol to autism and stated that "RFK Jr. and I understood a lot more than a lot of people who studied it." In most circles, an environmental lawyer or a real estate developer claiming vast medical expertise would be considered pathological hubris.

PART THREE

Trump's Second Term, as It Unfolded

CHAPTER 5

THE QUEST FOR UNLIMITED POWER: TRUMP'S WAR ON DEMOCRACY

May 23, 2025
Trump's War on Democracy
Dear Editors,

We appear to be in the midst of a battle for the soul and future of America—President Trump versus the Constitution and the founding principles of the United States. Namely, whether there are three equal branches of government and whether any man is above the law.

In addition to the global tariffs (deemed in court the proper province of Congress), this battle has manifested, among other things, in Mr. Trump's deportation of foreigners without due process (deemed in court a violation of habeas corpus), as well as his campaign to control law firms, newspapers, and universities.

Mr. Trump believes that a president has unlimited power. In his first term, he famously stated, "I have an Article 2, where I have the right to do whatever I want as president."

He recently doubled down by claiming that his election margin, just 1.5 percent of the popular vote, provides a mandate that supersedes any and all judicial oversight. In Mr. Trump's opinion, judicial oversight or judicial repudiation of his actions "undermines the democratic will of the people."

Trump's claim of unlimited authority violates the Constitution, goes against more than two centuries of precedence, and, most importantly, against the key principles behind the establishment of the United States: that no man is above the law, and that we do not abide kings. It has no basis in Article 2, in the election results, or anything beyond Mr. Trump's apparent self-entitlement and megalomania.

No president in the history of the United States prior to Donald Trump interpreted Article 2 anywhere even close to that manner, nor viewed their election results as putting them above judicial review. The implications are enormous. It is a war on democracy!

Mr. Trump has also argued in court that specific actions were justified by "national emergencies" (citing a critical trade imbalance, for his tariffs; a gang invasion, for mass deportations). Furthermore, he holds that a presidential declaration of emergency is not subject to review by Congress or by the courts. He alone decides what is and what is not a national emergency, and he alone determines the response to the perceived emergency. Can this be so? This gives presidents nearly unlimited power to do whatever they want based on an emergency that only they see.

The proper extent of presidential power will ultimately be decided by the Supreme Court. That worries those of us concerned over unlimited presidential power as this Court has already, via its previous immunity decision, declared the president essentially above the law. But Trump supporters should also be concerned. Every ruling in his favor, establishing unprecedented presidential power, will likely stand for the foreseeable future, and will apply equally for any Democratic president to come.

———————

May 24, 2025
Trump's South African Grift and Republican Hypocrisy
Dear Editors,

Richard Poplak's detailed and effective takedown ("A South African Grift Lands in the Oval Office," *New York Times*) of President Trump's misguided and misinformed intrusion into South Africa's affairs made me wonder how many presidents in the history of the United States before now inserted themselves into another country's internal governance in that manner, particularly involving a disputed issue (alleged prejudice against ethnic minority Afrikaners) with little to no ramifications for us? That seems in sync with Mr. Trump's extraordinary intrusion into and attempt to control our own civil society, dictating to private law firms who they can represent, to private universities what they can teach, to news programs what opinions they may air, to museums what they may display, firing people or eliminating programs he simply does not like, even declaring by fiat that the transgender identity does not exist. Nothing seems beyond Mr. Trump's self-perceived omnipotence.

At least Mr. Trump is not being hypocritical. This is who he has always been: compelled by accumulation of power, domination, and self-aggrandizement with complete disdain for any external limits, including the law, national (or state) sovereignty, personal privacy, and too many unintended consequences to list.

But what about the Republican Party? Their mission statement, their raison d'etre, has long been to limit big government and to prevent meddling in local or personal affairs or places outside of the circumscribed historical realm. Yet in response to Mr. Trump's unprecedented expansion of presidential and personal power—the antithesis of standard Conservative doctrine—Republicans remain silent or even applaud. Their hypocrisy is startling.

Mr. Poplak's op-ed critiques Mr. Trump; between the lines, it seems even more damning of the Republican Party.

———————

May 28, 2025
Trump's War on the United States
Dear Editors,

Today I read about President Trump suing the State of California over a transgender athlete, and the State of North Carolina over election lists, and reeling back all federal contracts granted to Harvard University. He also had both his withholding of federal funding from New York City (over a congestion pricing toll program) and his order targeting a private law firm (WilmerHale) dismissed by judges. Finally, he was sued by NPR and several Colorado radio stations over his executive order to block congressionally approved funds.

So far it is: Trump vs California. Trump vs North Carolina, Trump vs New York City, Trump vs Harvard, Trump vs NPR, Trump vs Colorado stations, and Trump vs WilmerHale.

All in one day. And it is only 9 AM.

Never in the history of the United States has a president waged war against so much of the United States.

———————

July 5, 2025
Trump's Lawsuits:The Guillotine Does Not Respect Justice
Dear Editors,

Paramount Global, CBS's parent company, just announced that it settled a Trump lawsuit against it based on the editing of an interview on the CBS News program *60 Minutes*. They did not admit fault or include an apology, but they coughed up $16 million. Most legal experts concluded that the suit had no merit.

Paramount was fearful about their potential liability ($20 billion!), and that bucking the vast power of the federal government was not worth taking the risk. Barry Diller, founder of Fox Broadcasting Company, described this elegantly, quipping that even though "the idea of setting this idiotic suit is horrible [...] It is understandable to bend the knee if there's a guillotine to your head."

This follows a slew of defendants settling cases that appeared to have no legal merit, yet would have been enormously costly to defend and included huge liabilities. These include The Walt Disney Co, parent of ABC, also for $16 million and Meta for $25 million.

Similarly, Paul Weiss and eight other law firms agreed to provide $940 million in pro bono work in order to avoid executive orders, heavy sanctions, and/or loss of security clearances. Columbia and Northeastern Universities have also capitulated to Trump's threats, with Harvard University in his sights and currently wavering.

These defendants capitulated, not because of the merits of the cases, but because even cases without merit have some small chance of succeeding, especially if they land in an unfriendly court. The potential liabilities—sometimes in the billions—are just too much to risk. They are, to paraphrase Diller, a guillotine at your neck.

Similarly, on a smaller scale, the Justice Department, or even just an extremely wealthy person (e.g., citizen Trump) can coerce an individual into a plea bargain or settlement simply on the basis of the legal fees. It is hard to contest a case if you cannot afford to do so, and for most people, standard legal fees are way beyond their means.

Long ago, Donald Trump found a weakness in the justice system—and he has pounced on it like a tiger on a gazelle, first as a wealthy private citizen, then as president with the powers and unlimited resources of the federal government—forcing others to capitulate to his demands, without regard to the merits of the case.

We now have a system where the Man in charge can get almost anything he wants by putting a financial or legal guillotine to the neck of anyone that opposes him. That includes large companies, law firms, universities, some foreign countries (in response to tariffs), and, worst of all, you and me. The guillotine does not respect fairness or justice; it never has.

This is not the legal system anyone intended. Or anyone would want.

——————————

July 6, 2025
Trump and TikTok: Does That Worry Anyone?
Dear Editors,

We just learned, via Freedom of Information Act lawsuits, how Attorney General Pam Bondi described and supported President Trump's denial of an established law that the Supreme Court had unanimously upheld.

This had to do with the Chinese company TikTok. Congress previously banned continued TikTok activity in the United States, requiring it to shut down or sell, due to national security concerns. The Supreme Court upheld the ban. But despite the Supreme Court's ruling, Trump ordered that the law not be enforced. He also offered complete immunity for anyone who had apparently violated the law, and additionally advised that they could continue to violate the law without incurring any legal liability. As Bondi described it, Trump decided that shutting down TikTok would interfere with his "constitutional duties" as well as his "core national security and foreign affairs presidential powers."

There is some legal leeway here for Trump, but no president has ever applied it even close to this extent.

Further, his own explanation is both contradictory and self-incriminating: Trump reinstated TikTok, the bipartisan Congressionally perceived threat to national security on the basis of national security! This tortured, convoluted explanation suggests some other unstated motivation, perhaps personal or financial interest.

I have little to no interest in TikTok, and this intervention did not generate much outcry from others. But today's news demonstrated how little to no checks and balances we have with regard to Trump's claim of unlimited power.

What can anyone do if Trump thwarts the will of Congress and annuls more laws?

Well, the Supreme Court could rule that he exceeded his constitutional duties. Given the current make-up of the Court, this seems unlikely.

As Trump sees it, any law that he wishes to overrule is actually within his constitutional duties and core powers as president. And this Supreme Court has established that they will give great deference to his own declaration of official agency and presidential powers. They are unlikely to rule against him. And even if they rule against him, the Supreme Court has no enforcement power.

Congress could, theoretically, impeach him, or use the power of the purse for enforcement purposes, but both seem unlikely except for truly extraordinary circumstances, and particularly for this Trump-controlled Congress.

Thus, it seems like the only thing holding Trump back from invalidating more laws in the future is his self-restraint and/or respect for the other two branches of government.

Does that worry anyone?

———————

July 18, 2025
The Maurene Comey Firing: The Tool of a Tyrant
Dear Editors,

President Trump's Justice Department just fired long-time federal prosecutor Maurene Comey. This was certainly Trump's call, as the notification letter to Comey cited his presidential authority, based on Article 2 of the Constitution.

No reason was given. Comey was one of the lead prosecutors in the currently white-hot Jeffrey Epstein case, though it is unclear whether or even why that would have prompted her firing. No other Epstein case prosecutor was fired.

Three other points leap out as possibly causative, as each characterizes Trump's standard operating procedure:

First, vengeance against all perceived enemies. Comey is the daughter of Trump arch-enemy James Comey. His daughter's firing, without obvious cause, reeks of a petty, childish, and even cruel slap in the face to Mr. Comey, an "any way I can hurt you, I will," action.

Second, the purging of non-sycophants. Maurene Comey, especially if she's anything like her dad, may have said something unflattering about or unsupportive of Trump, which he does not abide. That was suggested by Comey's public response to her firing, "Fear is the tool of a tyrant, wielded to suppress independent thought."

Third, Trump's micromanaging of American life. Why is he involving himself with a single prosecutor in New York, who few people had even heard of, and has not seemed to have done anything of significance other than her job? Is there anything too small or trivial for Trump to exercise his ever-expanding presidential powers?

What public or national interest is served by the president firing Maurene Comey? Or is it just the "tool of a tyrant?"

———————

July 22, 2025
Restoring Ethnic Slurs (in Sports)
Dear Editors,

Today's *Chicago Tribune* headline in the sports pages read "Trump wants sports teams to restore offensive names." That sounded so ridiculous, I chuckled—obviously, some kind of pun or joke. It reminded me of the famous *New York Post* headline "Headless Body in Topless Bar." But it turned out that the Tribune meant it! The next sentence read "President Donald Trump is threatening to hold up a new stadium deal for the Washington's Commanders NFL team if it does not restore its old name of Redskins, which was considered offensive to Native Americans."

In the event there was any doubt, White House press secretary Katherine Leavitt ended that, saying, "The President is serious. Sports is one of his passions [...] He wants to see the name of that team changed." This places Trump in the same boat as Redskins founder George Preston Marshall, who chose the original Redskins name in 1933, changed the team's fight song lyrics from "Fight for old DC" to "Fight for Old Dixie," and was the last NFL owner to integrate his team. Not good company to be in.

Trump also directed (this time, thankfully, without a threat) the Cleveland Guardians baseball team to return to its original name of Indians. And that followed his recent directive to rename Army bases to once again celebrate Confederate slaveholders and secessionists.

The Tribune's headline is not only serious; in several respects it is entirely in Trump's character. Trump is determined to reverse every iota of progress in cultural sensitivity and racial justice, even to the extent of restoring ethnic tropes and slurs. He is not just against the excesses of Diversity, Equity, and Inclusion (DEI); he is against DEI per se. In his worldview, diversity, equality, and inclusion are evil words. Trump seeks to return to a previous world when these ideas were mostly aspirational, and many folks were second-class citizens.

There seems no aspect of civilian life too small for Trump's presidential meddling—I mean, names of sports teams? This is the exact opposite of the Republican historical mantra that dictates government must stay out of local and personal affairs.

He will use the immense power of the presidency to obtain whatever serves his personal whims and interests, however trivial. He will even block a new stadium that is in the best interests of the community, in this case, returning a football team from Maryland to its historical home in the District of Columbia.

Seriously, restoring ethnic slurs to public prominence?

———————

July 28, 2025
Trump Against Jerome Powell: More War on Democracy
Dear Editors,

President Trump continues to feud with Federal Reserve chair Jerome H. Powell. Trump demands lower interest rates, but Powell refuses to act, including today, when he announced he was once again holding firm. His main issue appears to be an increase in the most recent annual inflation rate to 3 percent, well beyond the forecast of 2.2 percent, and generally thought to be due to Trump's tariffs.

As a noneconomist, I have no idea who is right or whether the best answer lies somewhere in between the two positions.

However, there seems to be a bigger issue in play here: Trump's attempts to intimidate Powell into capitulating. Much of that has just been public name-calling. Trump has called Powell "a moron […] just not a smart person […] a stupid person […] a golfer who can't putt […]. a numbskull […] too angry and too stupid." Trump then upped the ante by publicly decrying cost overruns on building renovations at the Fed, suggesting Powell was responsible, again hoping to intimidate him into capitulation. So far, Powell has resisted both the demand to lower interest rates and the demand to resign.

Which leads to the most worrisome part of this—Trump's recurrent threats to fire Powell. That is even more worrisome because the Fed is meant to be independent of the Executive Branch, among other reasons in order to allow the Fed to independently concentrate on long-term economic health. Politicians focus on the short term, particularly with regard to the effects of inflation on the next election.

Perhaps the threats are just an accessory to the name-calling, merely hoping to humiliate or intimidate Powell into resigning. But Trump commonly follows through on whatever appeals to him, so no one should be surprised if he does indeed fire Powell.

Powell is protected by the Federal Reserve Act, which says that the president can only remove Powell "for cause." This has been supported by a Supreme Court ruling in 1935 and by Samuel Alito, one of the Court's most conservative justices, in a footnote on a subsequent case, describing the Fed as "a unique institution with a unique historical background [...] a special arrangement sanctioned by history."

However, "for cause" is vague and subject to abuse. Obviously, if Trump ever fired Powell, he would cite a "legitimate cause." Who, if anyone, would then evaluate that? Would the Republican-led Congress stand up to Trump? Would the Supreme Court?

Or, would both accede to Trump's claim that he is the president, he gets to decide what "just cause" is, and his decision is immune from review.

If that is the way this goes down, then it will be a further erosion of our democracy.

————————

July 29, 2025
Trump's Deal With the European Union: Unfettered Power
Dear Editors,

Yesterday, President Trump announced a new trade deal with the European Union (EU). This was quickly touted as very favorable to the United States. However, the French prime minister called it a "dark day" and stated that the EU had "submitted."

If so, the EU likely submitted out of fear of a high tariff, exactly as Trump has suggested would happen.

However, before we exalt this deal as promoting our interests, there are a couple of things to keep in mind. First, tariffs have been applied to other countries and are allegedly responsible for the recent rise in the annual inflation rate to 3 percent. Additionally, the situations with Canada, China, and many other countries remain in flux. The net effect of all of this on our economy remains to be seen.

It certainly appears as if Trump coerced the EU into submission with a not so veiled threat—his usual modus operandi. Trump sees life as blood sport with winners and losers, with the goal of always being a winner by as much as possible and with no regard for the welfare of the foe. He is now extraordinarily powerful, not only because he is president of the wealthiest, strongest country in the world, but he also has an obeisant Congress, an obeisant Department of Justice, and a Supreme Court that commonly overrules federal court judgments restraining him. He is unfettered by the usual historical checks and balances.

That may have worked out well for us in this instance with the EU, but domestically, Trump has trampled the helpless and all sorts of people and institutions that have had no realistic choice but to succumb. That has included powerful media companies, universities, and law firms, not so powerful Latino immigrants, Muslims, and members of the LGBTQ community, women who have lost abortion access and child care services, Democrats or anyone affiliated with a Democrat policy, Republicans who have dared stand up to him (instantly labeled RINOs and likely to lose their seats), inspector generals, senior FBI officials, EPA employees, and career prosecutors. He has had free reign. Who is next?

A very powerful man in charge with no checks or balances, no concept of limitations, and who does whatever he wants. Sounds like a functional dictatorship!

————————

July 30, 2025
President Trump: You're No Jack Kennedy
Dear Editors,

Rep. Bob Onder (R-Mo.) is introducing a bill to rename the John F. Kennedy Center for the Performing Arts after President Donald Trump.

This recalls the comment made by Senator Lloyd Bentsen to Senator Dan Quayle in a vice presidential debate: "I knew Jack Kennedy [...]. Senator, you're no Jack Kennedy." Neither is President Trump.

Kennedy famously said, "Ask not what your country can do for you—ask what you can do for your country." Trump has famously lived his entire life asking what he can do for himself, and what others can do for him in his life's quest to acquire as much power, money, and advantage as possible, often at the expense of anyone or anything standing in his way.

JFK was honored based on his life-long celebration and support of the Arts. He viewed art as "[...] the great Democrat calling forth creative genius from every sector of society, disregarding race or religion or wealth [...]." He stated that "The new frontier for which I campaign in public life can also be a new frontier for American art." Furthermore, that "I look forward to an America which will reward achievement in the arts as we reward achievements in business and statecraft."

Kennedy had poet Robert Frost read a poem during his inaugural ceremonies, nationally promoting support of the Arts. He and Jackie then had a plethora of invited writers, painters, poets, and musicians perform at the White House, basically making the White House a national stage.

As for Donald Trump and the Arts? Not so much. Notably, Trump cut funding to the National Endowment for the Arts and the National Endowment for the Humanities.

What else can you call this but sheer obsequiousness on the part of Rep. Onder?

He wants to rename an art center for the purpose of gaining Trump's favor, perhaps getting a nice word said about him; better yet, support in his next election.

Few people really care about Bob Onder, or even know who he is, but his sad little ploy is a symptom of a larger problem: He is not the only one. Pretty much the entirety of Republican legislators are sycophants to Trump and in critical areas. For example, Senator Josh Hawley called Trump's Big Bill "immoral" then voted for it a short time later. Senator Lisa Murkowski loudly slammed the bill for harming her constituents, especially her poorer people, and then voted for it. Fifty Republicans just approved the appointment of Trump's personal lawyer, Emil Bove, to a lifetime appointment on the federal bench even though he had been roundly criticized for several episodes of prosecutorial misconduct.

Add to that a generally compliant and supportive Supreme Court.

When Trump said in his first term that "as President I can do anything I want," some folks laughed at his absurd read of Article 2 of the Constitution. Turns out that he was right and we are the laughingstock.

———————

July 31, 2025
Trump Stomps on Republican Dissent
Dear Editors,

President Trump's strive for unprecedented and absolute power was put on full display today when he excoriated two of his most loyal troopers: Senator Charles Grassley (R-IA.) and Senator Josh Hawley (R-Mo.). Apparently, it is not enough to be a Trump loyalist supporting almost everything he wants; you must support him 100 percent, 100 per cent of the time. Any slip, and you become a target of his ire.

Grassley is 91 years old; you would think that might earn him some deference, and he has been senator from Iowa for 44 years. As president *pro tempore* of the Senate, he was instrumental in getting several of Trump's most controversial appointees confirmed. Grassley's loyalty to the Republican Party and to Trump has never been questioned.

His malfeasance was to support an arcane procedure known as the Senate blue slip, which allows senators the final say in naming federal district judges and U.S. attorneys in their home states. This has been routinely used and supported by both parties for many years. A number of Republicans, including Senator Tommy Tuberville (R-Ala.), who usually is among the first to support Trump in any situation, defended Grassley's position.

But for Trump, losing even a tiny bit of control to local officials, even if that has been the norm seemingly forever, was enough to unleash a tirade in which he labeled Grassley a RINO, a standard Trump *ad hominem* trope that has been so overused it should have lost effect by now, and even called for his ouster.

Trump also attacked Hawley (R-Mo.), who voted for a bill banning inside trading by lawmakers, presidents, and vice presidents (sure seems reasonable). Hawley demonstrated his loyalty to Trump when he famously ran outside the Capitol with a raised fist to encourage the Jan. 6th rioters. More recently, after calling the Big, Beautiful, Bill "immoral," he flipped his vote to allow passage and a Trump victory. Like Grassley, his pro-Trump credentials were heretofore impeccable.

Trump was angered because the revised bill deleted Trump arch-enemy Democrat Nancy Pelosi's name. Trump has been urging an investigation of Pelosi's husband for insider stock trading although, at least publicly, Trump has provided no evidence of impropriety, and Pelosi actually has supported the bill.

Trump labeled Hawley's vote as "sabotage" and called him a Democrat "pawn," perhaps an even more malicious moniker than RINO.

There are several take-home points from Trump's back-to-back histrionics:

First, Trump is outraged by anything that decreases his power even one iota—in this case, something as low level as appointments of judges and attorneys at the state level. His quest for power seems to have no limits.

Second, he is relentless in his pursuit of his enemies.

Third, he demands total support from Republicans, and not even his staunchest loyalists are immune from his personal attacks.

No one is immune from Trump's attacks.

————————

August 6, 2025
Trump's Firing of the Labor Statistics Commissioner: The Medium Lie
Dear Editors,

President Trump's firing of the Bureau of Labor Statistics commissioner Erika McEntarfer was widely considered an expression of his underlying psychopathology, in which he fabricates enemies and conspiracies, rather than admit to his own slightest deficiencies—in this case, a poor jobs report.

However, there is another possible explanation. That is, Trump is fully aware that the reported job data was correct and his entire "rigged" story was just a lie, not one at the level of the Big Lie, but, perhaps, a "medium lie."

What would be the point of that? Probably not just to defend himself from a bad report, because almost everyone knows the truth. Many involved in the process came out publicly stating that a large number of people participated in generating the data and that McEntarfer could not possibly have altered the data without everyone knowing.

If Trump knew his claim to be false, then the firing of McEntarfer likely served to send a simple, if not ominous, message to all government employees, appointees, and career civil servants. That message is: If the truth you tell is not what Trump wants to hear, you might be fired.

This is yet another attempt, via overt intimidation, to expand Trump's power in every way conceivable, to control every employee in government, to have them do their jobs while preoccupied with satisfying his interests, even if at the expense of their honesty.

This comes straight out of the autocrat's handbook.

———————

August 7, 2025
Trump's Third Term: Believe It
Dear Editors,

Earlier this year, President Trump responded to a question about a possible third term by saying, "They do say there's a way you can do it." On another occasion, he said that it would be "the greatest honor of my life to serve not once, but two or three or four times." Yesterday, he again suggested that a third term is plausible, "I'd like to run. I have the best poll numbers I've ever had."

In fact, a recent Gallup poll reported Trump's approval rating at a near low for him of 36 percent.

Trump has waffled on this point, but he keeps his third term fantasy alive. Any other president would have given a hard "NO! End of discussion" response.

The Constitution seems to forbid a third term, but [...] Trump could declare a national emergency empowering him to continue as president. He has already declared a National Emergency at the Southern Border, a National Energy Emergency, and a National Emergency regarding our "National and Economic Security." It is a tactic he uses to pursue his goals.

A declaration of national emergency should, of course, require an actual national emergency. But the definition of national emergency is vague. The National Emergencies Act provides a framework, but not a specific definition of an emergency.

This vagueness manifested when Trump declared that trade deficits constituted an emergency that allowed him, rather than Congress, to levy tariffs. However, many economists do not consider trade deficits a significant problem. Furthermore, Trump's tariffs on India, for buying Russian oil, and on Brazil, for prosecuting a pal of his (ex-president Bolsonaro), clearly demonstrate that at least some of the tariffs have nothing to do with trade deficits. Thus, his national emergency claim is both idiosyncratic and debatable.

Who is right? More importantly, who decides?

Not surprisingly, there are ongoing lawsuits evaluating Trump's claim that trade deficits are a national emergency and the legality of his tariffs. They will end up in the Supreme Court, which will decide how much leeway and authority Trump has in this matter.

This Supreme Court, to say the least, has been very deferential to his executive power. No one should be surprised if they rule that Trump's judgment on the trade deficit national emergency cannot be challenged—that it is the president's call—or define standards that make it very difficult for Trump to be challenged.

In that event, Trump would have impetus and legal backing to declare a national emergency which would empower him to stay on as president in 2028, and it is doubtful that anyone could stop him. The objections from legal scholars would be impotent in the face of a Supreme Court guideline favorable to Trump.

With this president, backed by this Supreme Court, a third Trump term is no fantasy—it is a possibility.

March 7, 2025
Trump Versus the FBI: Turning Justice on Its Head
Dear Editors,

Today, FBI agent Brian Driscoll announced that he had been fired from his position at the bureau. Prior to that, Driscoll had a long, distinguished career at the FBI, marked by receiving the FBI Medal of Valor and the FBI Shield of Bravery, and being appointed as acting director earlier this year by President Trump.

This followed the recent firing of Steven J. Jensen, the head of the FBI's Washington field office. Jensen was fired for his role in responding to the insurrection at the Capitol. He had previously been lauded by Trump's current FBI director, Kash Patel.

Similarly, Driscoll was fired because he refused to hand over the names of FBI agents who had worked on the investigation into the Capitol attack. By doing so, he was protecting a large number of public servants from Trump's retribution. Most of us saw Driscoll's act as honorable, but it cost him his career at the FBI.

Trump is turning justice on its head: He pardoned the Jan. 6 criminals and is getting rid of, and possibly subjecting to legal action, a panoply of law enforcement agents and prosecutors who simply did their jobs in investigating or prosecuting alleged crimes, almost all of which ended up in plea bargains or convictions.

The criminals go free, law enforcement gets punished!

The firings of Driscoll and Jensen, among others, cannot be good for morale at the FBI. Nor for recruitment. Nor for current agents to be able to perform their duties without fear of political retribution and repercussions, including losing their jobs. It cannot be good for the FBI. And it is not good for America.

However, it is good for President Trump, which, in his mind, supersedes and overrides all else. As he purges the FBI and other agencies of people he dislikes or distrusts, he sends a message to everyone, everywhere, that no one should cross him, or there will be consequences.

This is the wrath of Trump in action.

—————————

August 14, 2025
Trump Runs Baseball, and Museums, and Performing Arts [...] No More Limits
Dear Editors,

Yesterday, President Trump announced this year's list of Kennedy Center honorees for excellence in the performing arts, which included George Strait, Michael Crawford, Sylvester Stallone, Gloria Gaynor, and the rock band KISS.

This was actually news, but not for the usual reasons.

First, the nominees had to satisfy a new requirement, never before even thought of. The honorees had to be Trump fans, or at least not "too woke." As Trump stated, he picked the honorees and he "turned down plenty because they were too woke."

Trump picked the honorees because, earlier this year, he fired the board of trustees due to their "wokeness" and replaced them with his friends and supporters, and then he took over as Chairman of the Board.

One might wonder why the president of the United States is spending time managing a Center for the Performing Arts. Not only because he surely has more important things to do, but also because this is an intrusion into a local matter that historically has been left to other people to manage.

Actually, the takeover of the Kennedy Center echoes standard Trump behavior.

Earlier this year, he interceded to get the storied baseball player Pete Rose reinstated to Major League Baseball, in order to restore Rose's eligibility for baseball's Hall of Fame. Rose had been given a lifetime ban in 1989 for gambling on games, including some that he managed. He remained banned, and thereby ineligible for induction, for the past 36 years, and under four separate Commissioners of baseball.

The current Commissioner, Rob Manfred, had been a strong critic of Rose throughout his 10 years in service. Then, Trump called for Rose's reinstatement and, just like that, Manfred had a change of heart. For sure, no coincidence. The only remaining question is how much intimidation and threat Trump applied to get Manfred to reverse his long-held stance.

Sometime after that, Trump banned the Smithsonian Institution from showing exhibits that he did not like. The Trump administration is now conducting a formal internal review of eight Smithsonian museums to ensure they follow the Trump directive that they "remove divisive or partisan narratives." That will be guided by Trump himself. And since he has the power and influence to pull much of the Smithsonian's financing, the Smithsonian leaders will likely follow his directives. In other words, he has declared himself the de facto Chairman and CEO of America's national museum. Trump is now basically running the Smithsonian, as he is running the Kennedy Center for the Performing Arts. First baseball, then art and history, then the performing arts.

There is more yet, but for brevity's sake, let's just note that Trump has attempted to influence, or has intervened in private companies (e.g., Coca-Cola, Nvidia, U.S. Steel), private universities, and even football teams. Trump is micromanaging, when it suits him, aspects of day-to-day life that have nothing to do with governance and cannot be said to be of national import.

There once was a day when almost all of quotidian life in America was considered exponentially beneath presidential intervention, and individuals and local institutions were allowed to make their own decisions. The central government stayed away, far away. The Republican Party once considered that important.

That day is over, those limits are gone.

———————

August 29, 2025
Trump's War on the Federal Government: A Very Bad Day for Democracy
Dear Editors,

President Trump's war on the federal government accelerated over the last twenty-four hours. First, he fired Lisa Cook, a Federal Reserve board member. Then, the administration placed 36 FEMA employees on leave, and, finally, at RFK Jr.'s request, Trump fired Susan Monarez, his own, and very recent, appointee as director of the Center for Disease Control and Prevention (CDC).

Imagine targeting FEMA, the Fed, and the CDC all in one day. That is an ambitious day!

If all of this stands, America will be more susceptible to natural disasters, to infectious diseases, and, according to many economists, to increased inflation and economic instability.

Cook was fired on a flimsy, and likely illegal, pretense. A Trump official alleged that she had committed mortgage fraud years ago. Trump claimed that this mere allegation, from a Trump loyalist, was grounds for firing even though such a dismissal, by law, can only be "for cause." "For cause" has historically required something directly related to professional activity, and not merely an allegation of a prior, unrelated, private act. Furthermore, the Supreme Court recently wrote in an opinion that the Fed's independence is crucial, unique among federal agencies, suggesting that the standard applied to "for cause" termination at the Federal Bank is even higher than for all other agencies. Trump will soon be asking the Court to rule against its own position of record.

Trump was forthright about his motivation behind this apparently illegal firing, stating that "Now we will have a majority on the Fed board," meaning that he can now direct the board to adjust interest rates at his discretion. In other words, if this firing stands, Trump will now function as the de facto director of the Fed.

The FEMA layoffs owed to a letter 182 current and former employees sent to Congress warning that various Trump actions had imperiled disaster response capabilities. It would seem that they are the very ones with the expertise to understand this, but Trump's response was to get rid of them, adding to previous FEMA firings.

Monarez's firing was not surprising. After all, at her confirmation hearings she stated that "vaccines save lives—this is an indisputable, well-established, scientific fact," that she saw no link between the measles vaccine and autism, and that fluoridated water was safe. The amazing thing is that she got nominated and confirmed with views that were antithetical to those of her future boss, RFK Jr.

As it turned out, she was fired less than one month into her term, precipitated, in large part, by her opposition to the FDA's new restrictive COVID-19 vaccine policy. The American Pediatric Association, the American College of Obstetricians and Gynecologists, and multiple other leading medical groups also declared their opposition to the new policy, so she was not alone in her conclusions.

Four top CDC officials immediately resigned in protest of her firing, one of them stating that "I am unable to serve in an environment that treats the CDC as a tool to generate policies and materials that do not reflect scientific reality, and are designed to hurt, rather than to improve, the public's health."

The leadership of the CDC has been gutted, losing five more highly trained, highly educated, upper echelon leaders at the behest of a retired environmental lawyer with no training or experience in public health or health care, who holds a variety of unfounded health care-related viewpoints. Those five, and perhaps others to follow, will be replaced by RFK Jr. clones, just as RFK Jr. replaced the previously fired 17 members of the CDC's vaccine advisory committee with clones. As RFK Jr. gains complete control of the CDC, so, too, does Trump, as RFK Jr. is his proxy.

The common feature of these firings is that no one is allowed to criticize President Trump or his policies. If you do, you are fired. Eventually, only Trump loyalists will remain in the Federal government.

It was a great day for Trump, akin to a sweep of a triple-header, increasing his control over the Fed, over FEMA, and over the CDC.

It was a very bad day for democracy in America.

———————————

September 15, 2025
Democracy in Peril
Dear Editors,

Among other important characteristics, democracy holds that no man is above the law and that the power of any elected official is limited. President Trump challenged that early in his first term, when he stated that the Constitution gives the president unlimited power. Yet, until he attempted to overthrow the government on Jan. 6, he did not really act in that manner. Jan. 6 was a pivotal moment, due to the unprecedented nature of the attempted power grab, as well as the Supreme Court's refusal to push back on it. SCOTUS delayed their immunity decision, allowing Trump to avoid trial, and then by their ruling, gave the president immunity for just about any presidential action.

Undoubtedly emboldened, Trump's second term has differed markedly from his first term. He has engaged in multiple unique actions, each characterized by three steps. First, Trump does something far beyond the previously accepted limits of presidential authority. Second, he justifies that by declaring an emergency situation. Third, he states that his declaration is inviolate, not subject to review by anyone. If you can declare anything an emergency, and then do anything you want based on the self-declared emergency, what you have is a roadmap for unlimited power.

Here are just a few examples:

1) He declared a national emergency at our southern border to justify mass deportations without due process. This included allowing ICE and other federal agents to detain Latinos on the basis of their ethnicity, which appeared to be an overt violation of the 4th amendment ban on unreasonable search and seizures. This recalled our sordid history of police pulling blacks over for "driving while black." Yet, the Supreme Court recently ruled in favor of this policy, eschewing checks and balances.

2) He declared an emergency in Los Angeles in response to circumscribed demonstrations against deportations. Local authorities and law enforcement felt they had this under control, but Trump, nevertheless, sent in both the marines and the National Guard. A federal judge ruled that Trump violated the law that forbids federal troops from engaging in civilian law enforcement. This is now in the Court of Appeals.
3) Related, he declared a "violent crime crisis" in the District of Columbia, took over the police force and mobilized the National Guard there as well. That was done even after the incidence of violent crime in D.C. had decreased, and even though no president, including Trump, ever deemed D.C. an emergency crime crisis area even when the incidence of violent crime, over at least several decades, was higher than it is now. No local authority, either political or in law enforcement, deemed D.C. crime an emergency requiring federal troops.
4) He levied tariffs, some quite extraordinary, even though that is considered the province of Congress. He justified that, in arguments for a case pending at the Supreme Court, by stating that he had declared a national economic emergency, that the president can make that judgment, and that it cannot be overridden by anyone.
5) He recently served as judge, jury, and executioner, ordering the killing of 11 individuals aboard a vessel in the Caribbean. He alleged that these individuals were drug dealers, de facto terrorists, and members of the Venezuelan gang Tren de Aragua (which Venezuela denied). He labeled this an "armed conflict" which allowed the rules of war to apply, meaning that he could have these people killed at his discretion. Categorizing unarmed, suspected drug dealers in international waters as wartime combatants threatening the United States seems beyond the pale. Historically, the Coast Guard arrested drug smugglers at sea; they were tried in courts as per accepted procedures, and, since drug dealing is not a capital crime, none of them are executed. Many legal experts considered Trump's killings as presidentially sanctioned murder.

Through various declarations of national emergency, Trump has claimed the power to send the National Guard to any city of his choice, to replace Congress as the proper assessor of tariffs, to engage in historically considered illegal searches and seizures, and to deport and even kill without due process. All of this is unprecedented, perhaps even heretofore unimagined.

To date, Congress has shown no interest in providing checks and balances. The Supreme Court gave Trump near-complete immunity from prosecution and has upheld several of his actions. The Democratic concept of co-equal branches of government has gone up in smoke.

Trump is now routinely extending his presidential authority far beyond that of any president in American history, into areas previously considered completely off-limits for a president, and without any limitations or consequences.

Yes, democracy is in peril.

CHAPTER 6

IMMIGRATION AND MASS DEPORTATION

March 19, 2025
Power Without a Shred of Wisdom
Dear Editors,

Socrates reportedly said, "Knowledge is power, but wisdom is knowing how to use it." That distinction appears to apply to the recent deportation of kidney doctor Rasha Alawieh.

I am also a kidney doctor. I do not know Doctor Alawieh personally, nor do I know any details about her case other than what has been reported in the media. But I do know that she is an expert in kidney transplantation, a vital, difficult, and highly specialized area; she is one of only three transplant nephrologists in the state of Rhode Island. She will not be immediately replaceable and the many patients she takes care of—sick patients on dialysis, or with kidney transplants—will suffer from her absence. Furthermore, she is highly regarded by her colleagues who have uniformly described her as a hard-working, talented physician.

It is alleged that she holds political beliefs that the Trump administration and others find abhorrent. Understood. But in the absence of actual activity—which has not been alleged—she represents no harm to others. Thus, her deportation will provide no benefit to anyone, whereas it will provide tangible and significant harm to many Americans. The imbalance here is huge.

Her deportation is an expression of power, applied without a shred of wisdom.

———————

April 18, 2025
Trump Bows to El Salvador
Dear Editors,

President Donald Trump refused to comply with a court order to "facilitate" the return of Abrego Garcia from an El Salvador prison. When El Salvador denied Mr. Garcia's release, Mr. Trump proclaimed that he was now "powerless." In virtually all other situations, Trump claims or at least tries to exert his power as much as he can, for example, by threatening to or actually levying punitive tariffs. Why does he not threaten El Salvador with a tariff in order to force Mr. Garcia's release?

He appears to be applying his vast powers only when and where they suit his personal interests, and ignoring court orders as he sees fit.

———————

June 14, 2025
Trump's War on Immigrants: Who Will Take Care of Grandma and Grandpa?
Dear Editors,

President Trump's recent admission about the value of undocumented immigrants in the agricultural and hospitality businesses should make one wonder: In how many other businesses are immigrants essential? What other specific problems will accrue should Trump continue to deport these people without any nuance or wisdom? What are the unintended consequences of Trump's compulsion to deport?

As a physician, I know that we already have a shortage of direct care workers—home health aides, personal care aides, certified nursing assistants, and others. These people care for the frail elderly, assisting with household chores, bathing, dressing, toileting, thereby allowing older adults, and even younger adults with disabilities, to remain at home, rather than end up in nursing homes. As the population is aging, the direct care shortage is predicted to grow to almost 900,000 by 2032, and that prediction came before Trump began his massive deportation initiative.

Almost 40 percent of these workers are currently noncitizens, about half of those are undocumented, with the latter proportion growing. These are difficult, low-paying jobs that do not attract either American citizens or skilled immigrants. As the current undocumented direct care workers are deported, they will be just about impossible to replace.

If this continues, one predictable result of Trump's poorly thought-out deportation project will be a whole lot of Americans asking, "Who's going to take care of grandma and grandpa?"

———————

June 15, 2025
Will Trump Admit Error?
Dear Editors,

Clarence Page ("When the president's peacemaking efforts invite more chaos," in the *Chicago Tribune*, June 15) opined that President Trump's exclusion of farm workers from deportation was simply in response to the needs of Trump-voting MAGA farmers, and not an admission of error. Hopefully, Page is wrong, and the new policy reflects a re-calibration, in which Trump eventually realizes that there is nothing unique about farm and hospitality workers as immigrants, that many of the immigrants he has deported and targets for deportation are good hard-working people contributing to America. Like my great-grandparents who immigrated over a hundred years ago to escape religious persecution in Tsarist Russia, many escaped dire circumstances at home and arrived here (legally or not) nearly penniless. With a good work ethic and aspirations for a better future, they ended up as good neighbors and respected, contributing members of their communities.

If Trump realizes this and focuses, as he originally stated he would, on deporting high-level criminals, this will be a major and welcome change. It will also be a concession that Trump realizes that he was wrong all along, and his opponents were correct; that good immigration policy, like any policy, should include wisdom, common sense, and decency. Good policy does not proceed mindlessly with a blow torch, irrespective of the harm caused to human beings.

What are the chances Trump will admit he was wrong?

———————

June 30, 2025
The Problem With "All's Well That Ends Well"
Dear Editors,

President Donald Trump often states that his deportation plan concentrates on deporting "violent, barbaric" criminals. That would make sense, as nobody wants to keep violent and barbaric immigrant criminals in this country. Of course not! But he himself puts the lie to that when he provides quotas for daily deportations, numbers that do not distinguish between known violent criminals, low-level criminals, possible criminals, and completely innocent people just caught in Trump's "fire first, aim later" approach.

Today's *Chicago Tribune* described two awful situations that arose from Trump's monomania. We learned of the deportation of a 64-year-old grandmother who had been living in the United States for 47 years, raising a family, not bothering a soul. Current ICE policies and procedures apparently do not contain the shred of wisdom or common decency that it would take to leave this poor lady alone. My goodness, a grandmother!

We also learned of Cheikh Fall's mistaken arrest by ICE. Fall is married to an American citizen and is not suspected of any crime. The arrest turned out to be an error and Fall was ordered released by a judge. ICE's mistake caused him to suffer 23 days of incarceration. This recalls, among others, the Columbia student Mahmoud Khalil, who was imprisoned for three months before ordered released by a U.S. federal judge.

"Ends well" does not mean that "all's well"—there is immense damage done in the process. In a moral and decent world that would evoke a whole lot of empathy and common-sense effort to make sure these things do not ever happen again.

Sadly, that is not happening.

——————————

July 1, 2025
Immigrant Detention Centers as Deja Vu
Dear Editors,

We have heard recently about the brutal conditions at immigration detention centers in general. I am not talking about the horrors of the prison in

El Salvador, but about the conditions in President Trump's detention centers in this country. The centers are already 15,000 inmates above maximum capacity, and reports keep coming out describing massive overcrowding, lack of access to food and showering, absence of basic medical care, poor sanitation, and more. Paul Chavez, litigation and advocacy director at Americans for Immigrant Justice in Florida, recently said, "These are the worst conditions I have seen in my twenty-year career. Conditions were never great, but this is horrendous."

The Trump administration is making no attempt to improve this situation. There appears to be a complete lack of interest in the plight of the imprisoned.

Should we be surprised? This is the same president who, in his first term, presided over the placement of immigrant children into cages in Texas. Trump had to be practically begged to end this, and when he finally did, he did little to actually try to reunite the many children so cruelly and intentionally separated from their parents.

The current conditions in immigrant detention centers are simply deplorable, a national disgrace, and should keep up all up at night.

———————

July 4, 2025
Trump Loves His Alligators
Dear Editors,

Yesterday, President Trump made a public visit to a new detention center just established on an old airstrip in the Florida Everglades. This is welcome—any new cells that reduce overcrowding and help these people get the nutrition, hygiene, and medical care that any human being deserves is a good thing.

However, the new center is surrounded by miles of swampland populated by alligators, leading Republicans to call it "Alligator Alcatraz." Perhaps we can give them the benefit of the doubt and just call that a really bad alliteration, but as for Donald Trump—in a press conference, he went on and on with great glee, discussing the possibility of alligators eating people attempting to escape. Among his cringe-worthy comments were "We're going to teach them how to run away from an alligator if they escape prison [...] don't run in a straight line [...] and your chances go up one percent." He also noted cheerfully that alligators "come cheap" in comparison to the salaries of human prison guards.

You actually had to see the press conference to understand how gleeful Trump was in discussing the possibility of alligators eating people. He saw this as great humor.

Trump loves his alligators.

———————

July 10, 2025
Birthright Citizenship: Don't We Want More Children?
Dear Editors,

President Trump is trying hard to end the birthright citizenship bestowal that has been in place for more than 150 years and previously upheld by the Supreme Court. The Court basically ruled that the phrase in the 14th Amendment conferring citizenship to "All persons born or naturalized in the United States" overrides the subsequent "[...] subject to the jurisdiction thereof." Despite that, Trump interprets the latter to exclude persons born to noncitizens in America.

The Supreme Court's ruling, at least for Conservative justices, is consistent with their usual deference to original intent. If the amendment intended to exclude children born in America to noncitizens from citizenship, that would have been written quite clearly. For example, that citizenship is bestowed on "All persons born in America except to non-citizen parents [...]," or, "[...] Only to children born to at least one parent with American citizenship [...]." To argue otherwise, you have to ascribe colossal carelessness to the very smart, extremely careful amendment writers. That seems preposterous.

The current Supreme Court is going to re-litigate this, and we will see if the six Conservatives hold to their usual deference to original intent, or jettison that in support of President Trump.

However that plays out, it still leaves this question: Why don't we want these children? They are as innocent as could be, and they are just as likely to grow up as responsible adults making solid contributions to American society as anyone else. Moreover, we need children: The birth rate in the United States hit a record low in 2023, with very bad implications for the workforce and the economy as a whole. And with the current Trump anti-immigration monomania, we can expect immigration to decline in the near future, exacerbating workforce shortages.

Some of these birthright children could end up as high achievers, for example, ex-South Carolina governor and presidential candidate Nikki Haley, or Olympic skating medalist Michelle Kwan. And others could do the sorts of jobs Americans generally will not do: work on farms, in the hospitality business, in direct patient care fields, and many others like that. These children are not the entire solution to our workforce problems, but every little bit helps. And they are innocent children who have done nothing wrong.

Recognizing the baby deficit, President Trump actually proposed paying women (though, merely a pittance) who have children, a so-called "baby bonus." U.S. women seem to have scoffed at that, with good reason, but it does illustrate an awareness of the problem.

Trump's intent to deport these children is obviously part of his war on immigrants. Given the long precedence, the previous judicial rulings, and our declining birth rate, the battle against birthright citizenship seems both uncaring and self-injurious.

———————

July 26, 2025
Is Trump Separating Children From Their Families Again?
Dear Editors,

The latest ICE data have been released, covering nearly six months of deportations, which allows us to determine whether ICE has been hewing to President Trump's promise to target criminals, "the worst of the worst [...] vicious and bloodthirsty." The answer is [...] not so much, and getting worse.

Of approximately 100,000 deportees since this process began, less than 15 percent had committed the sorts of crimes mentioned by Trump and colleagues: sex offenses, homicide, assault, kidnapping, and gang activity. Most of the criminal records cited consisted merely of traffic or immigration offenses. Many deportees had no criminal record at all!

Worse yet, the proportion of deportees with no criminal record—again, per ICE's own data—has zoomed up lately. Since May 25, 44 percent had no record.

The deportation of those with criminal records is widely understood and not controversial. As for the rest, several questions must be addressed:

1) Deportation of people without criminal records ruins the lives of human beings, fractures families, and removes many respected and productive members of American communities. What is the point? The goal? Is it just to pad the numbers so Trump can eventually brag about the huge success of his program? Are the numbers of actual immigrant criminals—the rapists and murderers and drug dealers that Trump so commonly talked about infusing our country—actually much less than his rhetoric promised? Was all that talk just empty hyperbole?
2) Why are deportations of people without criminal records increasing? Aren't we supposed to learn from early mistakes and improve, not get worse?
3) Worst of all, what happens to the innocent children, some of whom are American citizens, when their parents are deported? Are they taken with their parents, removing them from the only homes, schools, and friends they have ever known?

How many of these children were left behind, perhaps with other family members or put into foster homes? That is, mom and dad are "here today, gone tomorrow."

It sure looks like the Trump administration is once again separating children from their families!

———————

August 21, 2025
The Wall Again? Black Paint? Oy Vey
Dear Editors,

Earlier this year, President Trump revived his failed first-term plan to build a wall along our almost 2,000-mile-long southern border. The recent "big beautiful" budget bill allocated $50 billion for this purpose.

As a follow-up, the secretary of the Department of Homeland Security, Kristi Noem, just announced that, at Trump's request, the entire wall will be painted black, on the basis that the increased temperature of a black wall will prevent illegal immigrants from climbing over it.

There are so many problems with this!

The wall was considered such a bad idea in Trump's first term that his Republican-led Congress refused to fund it. And, of course, Mexico, despite Trump's persistent bombastic and absurd claims, refused to pay. Thus, very little new wall was built. Trump now has a rubber-stamp Congress, but that does not change a bad idea into a good idea.

One reason it is a bad idea is that a wall is only modestly effective. During Trump's first term, the limited wall was breached approximately 1,000 times a year, mostly using inexpensive power tools. Perhaps, years later, the new wall will be more sophisticated. In that case, asylum seekers will make their own adjustments. Many of them are determined to enter this country.

More importantly, the wall is not needed. Give Trump credit: illegal crossings have plummeted this year—without a wall—and he has already declared victory in this area. A problem that no longer exists does not need a solution.

Why is Trump throwing money away on an issue that has already been successfully addressed? Who knows? This may be an attempt to change history's judgment of his wall-mania as a failure, a promise not delivered, and this Trump cannot abide.

As for black paint? That is future material for a Saturday Night Live or South Park spoof. It is hard to imagine that Noem spoke with a straight face. The idea seems to be that after traveling hundreds of miles seeking entry into the United States, potential border-crossers will feel the black paint and say, "too hot, darn, we are beaten," and turn back. Rather than simply don gloves, or climb at night, when the black wall will be cooler.

Actually, it is even more nonsensical. Nobody climbs the wall hand over hand. The wall is too high and there is little to nothing to grip. Those who went over the existing wall used makeshift ladders; the color of the wall makes no difference to a ladder.

Black paint on the wall is the ultimate in show over substance. Apparently, Trump thinks a black wall looks great, or looks powerful, or something, but it has zero deterrence in preventing a breach.

Plus, painting the wall costs about $1 million a mile, or approximately $2 billion.

The same "beautiful" budget slashed money intended to feed hungry children.

It provided for lots of wall, lots of paint, but not so much food.

This makes no sense.

———————————

August 22, 2025
Trump's War on International Students
Dear Editors,

President Trump's war on international students goes hand-in-hand with his war on immigrants. It began earlier this year with the deportation of international students who expressed pro-Hamas sentiments or engaged in campus protests, viewed as anti-Semitic and dangerous by Trump. In doing so, the president ignored due process and any concept of freedom of speech, but at least he focused on a specific issue that had some legitimate concerns.

That appears to have exploded into a larger war on international students, many not associated with any threatening behavior. This includes a broadly applied maze of new obstacles to obtaining visas, and in some areas, a travel ban. As a result, those involved in higher education predict a 40 percent decrease in international student enrollment in American colleges beginning this semester. That is just short of Trump's goal. He has suggested a 15 percent quota on international students, representing a 50 percent decrease.

What could possibly be the point of that?

International students contribute significantly to both the intellectual discourse and the bottom line of our universities—they routinely pay full tuition, which provides scholarship money for American students.

Furthermore, almost half of our Fortune 500 companies were founded or co-founded by immigrants, contributing over $8 trillion a year in revenue and a huge number of jobs for Americans. Many of these entrepreneurs studied at American universities before they decided to stay.

These foreign-founded companies typically make great contributions to America. For example, both Moderna and Pfizer, which developed the COVID-19 vaccines that saved so many lives, were founded or co-founded by foreigners. Google and Tesla are also companies founded by foreigners. Other examples abound, too numerous to list here.

Former international students also help fill manpower shortages in important areas. For example, 20 percent of medical doctors in America are foreign; many stayed on in this country after completing their education here. And in my own field, nephrology, around 40 percent of new trainees in America are international. Without them, there would be a critical shortage of nephrologists (kidney doctors), as well as other medical specialties, in America.

The main explanation Trump has given for his war on international students is that they take up spots at Harvard that would have gone to American students. This is absurd, as it suggests that attendance at Harvard (which Trump is trying to cripple), or similar elite universities, is somehow needed for a productive life. Very few Americans attend elite universities, and those who qualify for admission to Harvard but are passed over for an international student invariably attend another excellent university and succeed in whatever they choose to do.

Any potential security concerns are belied by the nonselective nature of the current restrictions. After all, many of the international students, and many of the most talented, hale from India, hardly a hot bed of anti-American activity. Even outside of India, these are just kids seeking a good education, not hard-core militants. They can only help this country.

This particular manifestation of Trump's xenophobia is not only purposeless but harmful.

We used to believe that Immigrants Make America Great (IMAG). Apparently, not any more.

CHAPTER 7

RKF JR.

November 24, 2024
An Environmental Lawyer as Head of Health?
Dear Editors,

As a physician, I am as totally unqualified, by lack of training, knowledge, and experience, to head the Department of Justice as an environmental lawyer is in running the Department of Health and Human Services. Just the thought of me in that position is frightening, but at least I would not come to that job with an agenda of denying the value of basic and important law. In contrast, RFK Jr. believes that some of our greatest medical advances—vaccines for polio, mumps, measles, COVID-19—are essentially fraudulent, without merit, and dangerous. The equivalent would be if, in my application to head DOJ, I stated that the Bill of Rights, the right to vote, and the Civil Rights Act were nothing more than frauds perpetrated on an unsuspecting public by conspirators.

With zero qualifications and with groundless views like that, my application at DOJ would be rejected the moment it arrived.

———————

November 25, 2024
Fauci Says Everything We Need to Know About RFK Jr.'s Nomination
Dear Editors,

RFK Jr. gave a lecture at the NIH which was discussed by Dr. Anthony Fauci in an interview in my college alumni magazine. It is a small college, so the readership is limited. Fauci's recollections deserve far greater exposure.

RFK Jr.'s first slide reportedly read "It has been well established that vaccines cause multiple sclerosis, lupus, autism, rheumatoid arthritis, cancer, mental illness."

Every physician in the world knows this is the medical equivalent of "the world is flat" or "9/11 was an inside job." Then, as told by Dr. Fauci, "[…] He gave another 30 or 40 slides, all of which had no basis in reality. At the end of it, I concluded that I could not have a normal conversation with him […]. He violated all the principles of data analysis, evidence, and truth."

Dr. Fauci concluded by saying, "But I'm not going to say anything about his appointment."

Actually, Dr. Fauci, you just said everything anyone needs to know about RFK Jr.'s appointment.

———————

November 26, 2024
RFK Jr.: Total Nonsense
Dear Editors,

I strongly disagree with Dr. Cory Franklin's (*Chicago Tribune* op-ed writer) suggestion that RFK Jr. is a plausible candidate to head Health and Human Services, depending on how one balances his "strengths and weaknesses." First, citing his "undeniable strength" as "identifying critical problems" is damning with very faint praise. Almost everyone involved in health care is very well aware of the issues of autism, obesity, nutrition, financial conflicts of interest, and the like.

In contrast, RFK's "fabrications," as Dr. Franklin aptly calls them, about vaccines and a variety of other issues, are not merely benign points to be deemed as similar in nature and importance to his so-called strengths. This is a false equivalency.

Dr. Franklin writes that his "fabrications" are "total nonsense." While some of RFK Jr.'s concerns are laudable, they pale next to his "total nonsense."

"Total nonsense" should be immediate grounds for disqualification as our leader of national health policy.

———————

November 27, 2024
RFK Jr. and Pasteurization
(Published in the *New York Times*)
Dear Editors,

RFK Jr., recently chosen to lead the Department of Health and Human Services, is well-known for a collection of preposterous beliefs: among others, his anti-vaccine stance, his assertions that Human Immunodeficiency Virus (HIV) does not cause AIDS, and his advocacy of raw milk and demonstrably failed treatments like ivermectin, hydroxychloroquine, and chelating compounds.

Anyone who believes these are benign statements, mere differences of opinion, and would have no effect on Americans should RFK Jr. be confirmed ought to carefully read David A. Kessler's November 27 Opinion guest essay, "I Ran Operation Warp Speed. I'm Concerned About Bird Flu."

Specifically, Dr. Kessler notes: "California has recently seen a significant rise in detection of H5N1 in dairy herds [...]. That is why it is important to pasteurize milk, which kills the virus."

Should this virus mutate, as Dr. Kessler fears, and evolve to human-to-human transmission, RFK Jr.'s advocacy of raw milk will be deadly.

This is just one example of the actual damage that could accrue should RFK Jr. be confirmed.

———————

February 2, 2025
The Venal Deal Trump Made with RFK Jr.
Dear Editors,

It is generally an excellent idea for any newspaper to present both sides of an issue, but in the case of RFK Jr.'s nomination, the *New York Times* just "sane-washed" it. It treated an insane idea as if there were opposing rational sides, and in the process, provided harmful credence where none is deserved. Not every crazy idea warrants public discussion just because it exists; there are people who believe the earth is flat or the moon landing was a hoax, but no reasonable person considers the pros and cons of those views worthy of debate.

With any other president, RFK Jr. would not have been one of the top 10,000 candidates for the position of secretary of Health and Human Services.

The only way he could possibly be nominated for this position was in exchange—a *quid quo pro*—for dropping out of the presidential race and throwing his 2 percent support to Donald Trump.

That is, this looming threat to the American health system owes to a venal deal: Donald Trump enhancing himself at the expense of all others.

————————

February 25, 2025
Even His Family Thinks He Is Unqualified
(Published in the *Chicago Tribune*)
Dear Editors,

The problem with RFK Jr.'s confirmation as secretary of the Health and Human Services Department is not just that he believes many of the greatest achievements in modern science and medicine are essentially fraudulent—vaccines, HIV medicines, pasteurization, and flourodinated water. After all, he could, as he has, walk back these bizarre claims and promise not to follow his previous thinking. However, it still leaves one to ask: What kind of thought process leads to so many comically awful, evidence-less conclusions?

It is his thinking process that should scare all of us, not simply the awful details of his track record. That irrational thinking mode cannot be jettisoned at the drop of a confirmation. It defines the man and predicts the performance to come.

That is actually the warning that many members of his family, the people who know him best, sounded loud and clear.

———————————

March 28, 2025
We Have Met the Enemy and He Is Us
Dear Editors,

The old saying "be careful what you wish for" (or, in this case, vote for) appears to be playing out, at least in the political-medical sphere.

After President Trump appointed RFK Jr., RFK Jr. appointed his clone, David Geier, to head yet another study of the long-discredited vaccine/autism link. Geier has been an ardent advocate of this nonexistent cause and effect relationship. Among other concerning issues, Geier does not have a medical degree and has been disciplined by the State of Maryland's Board of Physicians for practicing medicine without a license. Only in Trump's America could someone like Geier, via someone like RFK Jr., be given this responsibility.

For certain, as Geier was specifically chosen for this purpose, he will eventually claim, however preposterous, to find a causal link between vaccines and autism, at least enough of a link to spur a large number of vaccine skeptics to refrain from vaccinating their children.

According to the CDC, in the decade prior to the 1963 vaccine, measles caused 400 to 500 deaths, 48,000 hospitalizations, and 1,000 cases of encephalitis every year. The measles vaccine essentially eliminated all of that until recently in Texas. And this was only after vaccination rates in Texas declined.

However, as sure as night follows day, after Geier's "study results" are issued, the administration of measles vaccinations, and others, will decline further, and children will once again suffer and even die.

In a sense, this is our doing. We elected Trump, and the appointments of RFK Jr. and then Geier followed an expected path. As voters, we too must assume responsibility.

This is no laughing matter but to some extent, as the comic strip Pogo famously said, "We have met the enemy and he is us."

———————

April 18, 2025
RFK Jr.'s Bizarre Thoughts on Bird Flu
Dear Editors,

Recently, the possibility of a bird flu epidemic arose.

Unfortunately, Robert F. Kennedy Jr. just advised allowing bird flu to spread through flocks of domestic birds. That is completely the opposite of the thinking of scientists in the field, which is that the bird flu virus "demands redoubling efforts to prevent its spread to humans," as explained in a recent *Chicago Tribune* op-ed by Drs. Robert Weinstein and Cory Franklin.

Hopefully, RFK Jr. will heed the advice of these two physicians and many others.

Otherwise, things may not go well for us.

———————

June 25, 2025
RFK's Autism Idiocy
Dear Editors,

Dr. Allen Frances comprehensively discussed "The Real Reason Behind the Increase in Autism," which is the broadening of its definition to include Asperger's syndrome, as well as an exquisitely increased awareness of the autism spectrum diagnosis, and not the thoroughly debunked and dangerous vaccine idea.

I wish RFK Jr. read the *New York Times*. Or consulted anyone actually in the field.

———————

June 28, 2025
The First "A" in MAGA is for America. Foreign Children Don't Count
Dear Editors,

RFK Jr.'s hand-selected members of the CDC's Advisory Committee on Immunization Practices just decided that "it would no longer recommend annual flu shots that contain thimerosal" ("Flu Shot Vote Signifies Full Circle for Kennedy On Vaccine Skepticism" *New York Times* 6/28). This was in obeisance to RFK Jr.'s stated belief that "500 peer-reviewed studies [...] virtually every one of them said that thimerosal is a potent neurotoxin that should not be in vaccines."

That is the opposite of the actual scientific evidence. Dr. Mehmet Oz, appointed by President Trump to run the Centers for Medicare and Medicaid Services, stated that any putative link has been "discredited." Dr. Walter Orenstein, previous head of the CDC's vaccination programs, noted that "mercury has never been linked to autism." The U.S. Food and Drug Administration stated that "A robust body of peer-reviewed scientific studies conducted in the U.S. and other countries support the safety of thimerosal-containing vaccines." The World Health Organization concurs. So much for RFK Jr.'s, and this administration's, intellectual honesty and heeding to actual evidence.

Regardless, thimerosal has already been removed, as a precaution, in nearly all vaccines used in the United States. For our purposes, this is essentially a non-event, basically, political posturing. In contrast, thimerosal is still used in the less expensive multi-use flu vaccines that poorer countries need for mass vaccination programs. As the dissenting member of the panel, Dr. Cory Meissner, a pediatric infectious disease expert, stated, the ban "Is going to reduce access to these vaccines and increase cost." That is particularly likely in view of President Trump's ending of the United States Agency for International Development (USAID) program, and its support of health care abroad.

With increased cost, decreased availability, and decreased use of vaccines abroad, surely some children outside of the United States will unnecessarily suffer and even die.

In Trump's MAGA acronym, the first "A" stands only for America. Sadly, it does not cover children in need abroad.

———————

June 28, 2025
RFK Jr. and Gavi: Stunning and Calamitous
Dear Editors,

Today we learned that RFK Jr. is ending funding to Gavi, a major international vaccine organization. Noted global health expert Dr. Atul Gawande called this "stunning and calamitous." In short, children will die.

This follows upon President Trump's decision to end funding for USAID, which provided humanitarian aid to Africa, including HIV prevention. Since then, with loss of access to HIV medicines, thousands of Africans have reportedly died, with more to follow.

Is there a point at which the Republican Party, especially elected officials, realizes this is no joke? People are dying as a result of their ignorance of science, pursuit of reelection at all costs, and fear of Trump's wrath.

Death should not be subject to or secondary to political interests.

———————

June 29, 2025
RFK Jr. Goes Beyond Woody Allen
Dear Editors,

The 17 people RFK Jr. chose to replace the professionals serving on the CDC's Vaccine Advisory Board were chosen based on their vaccine skepticism and the certainty that they would reinforce RFK Jr.'s anti-vaccine agenda. Today, however, we learned the comically awful extent of this horrible charade. One of the appointees is Dr. Robert Malone. Among his "qualifications" are his endorsement of hydroxychloroquine and ivermectin as treatments for COVID-19, his belief that Trump's COVID-19 vaccine caused a form of AIDS (oddly, at times Malone has claimed to be the inventor of mRNA vaccines), that the severity of the COVID-19 pandemic, which killed over one million Americans, was exaggerated, that Americans were hypnotized—yes, hypnotized!—into taking the vaccine, and, perhaps most insane of all, that much of the federal government's business is conducted via sexual favor!

I mean, you cannot make this stuff up: A guy like this receiving an important appointment making decisions that could affect all of us. If Woody Allen, or even Mad Magazine, wrote a spoof on politics and government like this, it would be rejected as too implausible to be accepted by the viewing public. After all, satire must be reality-based, and nobody would believe this.

But this is no laughing matter. As Dr. Fiona Havers, former medical epidemiologist and head honcho at the CDC, said of this developing story, "A lot of Americans are going to die." Because, as noted vaccine expert Dr. Paul Offit observed, "I think we are on the verge of losing vaccines for this country [...] and the reason is [...] Robert F. Kennedy Jr."

Which leads to this: RFK Jr. received this appointment in exchange for withdrawing from the presidential race and throwing his support—his two percent in the polling—to Trump. To be fair, this sort of noxious quid pro quo is not at all shocking for politics. But, in most cases, the person trading his support is given a position within his area of expertise. Or, an honorary position of little actual import, say, an ambassadorship to "name-some-small country."

That has not happened here. Donald Trump not only appointed RFK Jr. to one of the most important and impactful departments in our government, but he then gave him carte blanche to do whatever he wanted.

———————

July 10, 2005
Only Trump Can Save Us From RFK Jr.
Dear Editors,

Anyone who thought that the furor over Trump's RFK Jr. appointment was hyperbolic, or counterbalanced by RFK Jr.'s interest in food dyes and fast food, has been slapped in the face with today's report of the expanding measles outbreak, now 1,288 reported cases in 38 states. That is already the most cases in 25 years, with still half the year to go. Roughly 3 percent of pediatric measles cases are fatal, and many more cause severe illness and permanent disability due to measles encephalitis (inflammation of the brain). This is a major public health calamity.

To be fair, RFK Jr. is only one of many advocates whose vaccine antagonism prompted the recent decline in vaccination rates, resulting in most of these infections. However, his anti-vaccine agenda, and his appointments of like-minded people into important positions, are all cause for alarm going forward. And this is to say nothing of the ongoing support and approval of the president.

A recent study published in the respected medical journal *JAMA* found that if childhood vaccination rates decline by 50 percent in the United States over the next 25 years, we can expect 51.2 million cases of measles, 9.9 million cases of rubella, 4.3 million cases of poliomyelitis, and 197 diphtheria cases; this epidemic of preventable disease adds up to 10.3 million hospitalizations with 159,200 deaths. Wow.

RFK Jr. is too intransigent to change his thinking—his only reaction to the accumulating measles cases has been to tout unproven or ineffective treatments, rather than primary prevention. However, MAGA followers do respond to President Trump. Perhaps the president will be more open-minded in light of these recent events and dire predictions, and post something on social media like "LET'S PUT A HOLD ON THE AUTISM THING FOR NOW. PLEASE VACCINATE YOUR KIDS."

It is a long shot, but it seems like only President Trump can save us from RFK Jr.

————————

July 15, 2025
Just Walk Through Any Cemetery
Dear Editors,

One of the easiest and saddest ways to understand the absurdity of vaccine antagonism is, as Laurie Burgess notes in today's *New York Times*, to walk through a cemetery. We have all done that, and we probably can remember the sinking feeling in our bellies when we read the headstones of children who died. Historically, many of those tragic deaths were due to infectious diseases—diseases that have been prevented, and in some cases, eradicated by vaccination. But only if parents give their children the vaccines. Which they will do only if the vaccines are recommended.

Both President Trump and RFK Jr. should walk through their nearest cemetery and remember that vaccination keeps children safe.

August 6, 2025
RFK Jr., mRNA, and Dr. Frankenstein
Dear Editors,

RFK Jr. announced today that he is canceling 22 projects designed to develop mRNA vaccines for various respiratory illnesses, including COVID-19 and H5N1 (bird flu). He also announced that these "troubled mRNA programs will be replaced."

Prior to this, the development of mRNA vaccines was considered a great scientific advance by everyone in the field. In fact, Katalin Kariko and Drew Weissman jointly received the 2023 Nobel Prize for their pioneering work in this area.

The mRNA approach provided the mechanism behind President Trump's COVID-19 Operation Warp Speed, which produced effective vaccines in record time—truly one of the greatest medical accomplishments of the modern era. Non-mRNA vaccines, sometimes called whole cell vaccines, take substantially longer, often many years.

The rapidity of development helped the mRNA COVID-19 vaccines save many millions of lives worldwide, including at least several hundred thousand in the United States alone.

If RFK Jr., with President Trump's imprimatur, has his way here, when the next pandemic appears a large number of people will likely die waiting for a lifesaving vaccine to be developed. As such, noted infectious disease and public health specialist Michael Osterholm of the University of Minnesota said, "I don't think I've seen a more dangerous decision in public health in my fifty years in the business."

President Trump should realize that this is taking craziness and/or political posturing into the realm of killing people. This is not the place to make political points or to flex your muscles to feel and look good.

RFK Jr., in a position of authority, is wholly Trump's creation, a modern retelling of the Frankenstein story. It is Trump's responsibility to stop this before the damage is done.

———————

August 29, 2025
RFK Jr.'s New COVID-19 Vaccine Policy: Ignorance Is Dangerous
Dear Editors,

Under RFK Jr.'s guidance, the FDA recently issued a new COVID-19 vaccine policy. This was roundly panned by multiple leading medical organizations including, among others, the American Pediatrics Association and the American College of Obstetricians and Gynecologists, as well as the director of the CDC, Susan Monarez, who was summarily fired for her dissent.

The medical establishment has two issues with the new policy. First, that it is too restrictive with regard to vaccinating children and pregnant women. Second, the establishment objects to RFK Jr.'s demand that all new vaccines, under all circumstances, undergo placebo-controlled trials before being approved.

The latter demand makes a nice sound bite for RFK Jr. It makes him sound earnest, insightful, and well-meaning, but his demand actually is hypocritical, dishonest, unnecessary, and dangerous. Yes, all of that.

It is hypocritical because, while demanding the most rigorous scientific evidence to allow approval of future vaccines, he proclaims crazy ideas in other areas that have zero supporting scientific evidence. That is, he requires a high standard of proof for others, but no level of proof at all for himself.

It is dishonest because the vaccines he criticizes the most—the COVID-19 vaccines that he has called "the deadliest vaccines ever made," and the measles vaccines, among others—have been conclusively shown effective and safe by several placebo-controlled studies. In other words, while claiming, when it suits his purposes, that placebo-controlled trials are dispositive, he ignores or denies results from other studies using that same methodology.

His demand for placebo-controlled trials for vaccines is also unnecessary or dangerous, depending on the clinical context.

The role of this methodology in assessing new vaccines for new infectious diseases is taught in the first year of medical school and has long been a staple of modern medicine. The first placebo-controlled trial was done almost two centuries ago, and the polio vaccine was studied with a placebo-controlled trial 71 years ago. RFK Jr.'s demand here is unnecessary, merely bluster.

Worse yet, the policy will be dangerous if he can enforce the requirement for placebo-controlled trials to evaluate new vaccines that are potential upgrades to already existing vaccines. This is a wholly different situation than assessing a vaccine for a newly emerged disease, when you cannot know beforehand if the vaccine is effective or safe. The issue for a potentially more effective vaccine is whether the new vaccine works better than the old one, and the appropriate study is simply to compare the new vaccine to the old one. A placebo arm adds nothing, and providing placebos to study participants in these circumstances is dangerous. It leaves these people, for no justifiable reason, vulnerable to the disease in question, and some of the study participants receiving placebo will die from the disease. This violates the most basic medical ethics. RFK Jr. seems wholly unaware of this.

This is a perfect example of what happens when an environmental lawyer with no training or experience in medicine, science, or public health is put in charge of medicine, science, and public health.

Ignorance leads to ignorant policies. And ignorant policies can be dangerous.

———————

September 6, 2025
RFK Jr.'s Congressional Testimony
Dear Editors,

Among all of the disturbing commentary in RFK Jr.'s congressional testimony, several lowlights stand out.

First, Kennedy stated that he fired his own appointee, Susan Monarez, as director of the CDC because she stated, in response to a question, that she was "not a trustworthy person." At no time in her entire professional career, nor at her recent confirmation hearings, has anyone questioned her trustworthiness, but that is actually beside the point. Even the most untrustworthy person, if asked by her boss if she was trustworthy, would answer, "Of course, I am." So, this was a comically absurd fabrication by RFK Jr., yet told with a straight face to Congress and to a national audience. This removed even the slightest bit of credibility from anything RFK Jr. said the entire day.

Second, this was Louisiana Senator Bill Cassidy's chance to redeem himself. Cassidy is the physician who naively accepted RFK Jr.'s claim that his anti-vaccine zealotry had ended and cast the deciding ballot in RFK Jr.'s favor to advance his nomination out of committee. Obviously, Cassidy was played, and his questioning of RFK Jr. at the hearings demonstrated that he knows that. This was his chance to publicly rescind his previous vote, to ask RFK Jr. to resign, and/or to ask President Trump to fire him. Unfortunately, Cassidy did none of that. It is one thing to make a mistake; we all do, but failing to correct a serious error when given a golden opportunity to do so? Unforgivable.

Third, the unspoken question hanging over the room was whether President Trump will fire RFK Jr. in response to the growing uproar against him. After all, Trump had a revolving door for appointees in his first administration, so he certainly is not shy about firing people. However, none of those firings were for incompetence. They were all for perceived disloyalty to Trump or to his goals.

That is the context in which RFK Jr. was asked about Trump's Operation Warp Speed initiative, specifically, whether he agreed that Trump deserves the Nobel Prize for it. The question referred to RFK Jr.'s oft-stated claim that Trump's COVID-19 vaccine killed more people than it saved. To keep his job, he swallowed his pride and agreed that Trump was deserving. This was obviously disingenuous, but RFK Jr. knows that Trump is consumed with exaltation and does not abide criticism. If past predicts future, as long as RFK Jr. refrains from criticizing Trump, and unless the backlash to him becomes so overwhelming that it becomes injurious to Trump, his job is safe.

However, with RFK Jr. at the helm of health care, the rest of us are not safe.

CHAPTER 8

TRUMP'S OTHER APPOINTEES

December 4, 2024
Hegseth Will Stop Drinking!
Dear Editors,

President Trump recently nominated Pete Hegseth for defense secretary despite minimal qualifications and several misconduct allegations, including an alleged drinking problem.

However, during his private vetting sessions, Hegseth repeatedly promised senators that "My commitment is to not touch alcohol while I have this position," as related by Republican senator Kevin Cramer. This was affirmed by Senators Eric Schmidt and Roger Wicker.

I wonder if a candidate for a position said in an interview, "I promise to stop drinking if you hire me," how many of us would hire that person, for example, as part of your medical staff, or as an elementary school teacher, or on the school board, to babysit your children, or to manage your finances.

Or, would the comment be immediately disqualifying?

——————————

March 12, 2025
Shambolic and Incompetent
Dear Editors,

A remarkable thing about conservative writer Bret Stephens's *New York Times* expose ("Democracy Dies in Dumbness") of President Trump's "incompetence" and "shambolic nature" is that he easily made the points without including Trump's appointment of RFK Jr. to secretary of Health and Human Services. RFK Jr.'s first public action in his new position was to tout ineffective treatments for measles: Vitamin A and cod liver oil. This is reminiscent of Trump's advocating ineffective treatments for COVID-19 such as hydroxychloroquine, household bleach, and ivermectin, while at the same time keeping largely quiet about the vaccine that actually prevents the disease.

Stephens also did not need to cite placing Elon Musk—who believes that Social Security is "the biggest Ponzi scheme of all time" and that "the fundamental weakness of Western civilization is empathy"—in a position of power.

If you judge a man by the company he keeps, Trump has indicted himself.

—————————

July 1, 2025
Trump Endorses Multiple Personality Disorders
Dear Editors,

RFK Jr.'s new handpicked Vaccine Advisory Committee is starting to do its damage, and many experienced and talented people in the field fear that a disaster looms.

And RFK Jr. is only one of Trump's bizarre and dangerous appointees.

Consider, for example, Matt Gaetz, Representative from Florida, who Trump nominated for U.S. attorney general. Gaetz, an election denier, was investigated by the House ethics committee for sex trafficking, statutory rape, and drug use. Yes (you cannot make this stuff up), Trump's appointee for U.S. attorney general has actually been investigated for sex and drug crimes. Seemingly due to all the scandalous publicity and the chorus of Republican misgivings, Gaetz withdrew from consideration.

Trump then appointed Pam Bondi, who had once received a Trump illegal campaign contribution and, as one of her major "qualifications," defended him in his first impeachment trial. She was confirmed and quickly sued the states of New York and Illinois, as well as the city of Chicago, part of Trump's war on the United States.

Then there is perhaps the worst of all—not an appointee, but the same story in a different form—Trump's support of Trump-worshipping, former football player Herschel Walker for senator of Georgia (thankfully, Walker lost.) In his own memoir, Walker described himself as suffering from severe mental illness; specifically, a dissociative identity disorder which gave Walker 12 different personalities. One of those personalities—again, this is Walker's own telling—played Russian Roulette with a loaded gun. Another—or maybe the same one—was physically abusive to women. His ex-wife, Cindy DeAngelis Grossman, said that he put a gun to her head and threatened to "blow my brains out." Walker did not deny that.

Mr. Walker, of course, stated that his mental illness had spontaneously resolved. Psychiatrists cast doubt on that, but regardless, and with sympathy to Mr. Walker for his self-described affliction, can you imagine any politician in the history of the United States supporting Mr. Walker? With that mental health history, for such an important position? Mr. Walker's loyalty to Trump should go only so far, and in this case, it should have gone nowhere.

None of Trump's other second term appointments were quite that outrageous or unqualified, except maybe Linda McMahon, the professional wrestling executive who somehow became Secretary of Education. However, it is obvious that these people were not chosen specifically for their qualifications. None of them could plausibly make the case that they were the most qualified candidate available for their position.

What changed from the first term, when Trump's appointees were more qualified, to the second? The first term appointees often disagreed with Trump and prevented him from implementing some of his crazy ideas. They were then routinely fired and subjected to Trump's calumny.

Trump seems to have learned an important lesson from his first term: Appointments should not be made based on qualifications other than unwavering fealty. That has been the second term's gold standard.

———————

July 2, 2025
Emil Bove: Very, Very, Loyal
Dear Editors,

Today we learned more about Trump's appointment process, the preeminence of loyalty as a requirement, and the disregard of actual qualifications. The Senate Judiciary Committee just held a hearing on Trump's appointment of Emil Bove to serve as a judge on the United States Court of Appeals for the Third Circuit—a lifetime appointment. Bove, like Pam Bondi, has been Trump's personal lawyer and has served as an agent of Trump's vengeance.

For example, as acting deputy attorney general he ordered FBI officials to compile lists of agents who participated in investigations of the Jan. 6 rioters. Bove also fired Justice Department prosecutors who were hired to work on the Jan. 6 cases—apparently the crime committed on Jan. 6 was not the storming of the Capitol, but investigating and prosecuting those who did. Finally, he ordered prosecutors to drop criminal charges against New York City mayor Eric Adams in exchange for Adams cooperating with Trump's immigration agenda. You would think that instigating or dropping criminal charges on the basis of political interests would be basic violations of judicial ethics. But, apparently not for Bove.

Numerous former Justice Department lawyers, 915 to be exact, urged the Judiciary Committee to reject Bove's nomination, citing his "trampling over institutional norms."

More than 75 former federal and state judges also called on the Committee to reject Bove's nomination, noting that these instances "[…] reflect a troubling pattern of abusing prosecutorial discretion to shield political allies." These judges also stated that "It is deeply inappropriate for a president to nominate their own criminal defense attorney for a federal judgeship, especially when that president has said he is nominating judges based on whether they will be more loyal to him than the country."

Trump disagrees. That is exactly the reason he nominated Bove: He is very, very, loyal.

———————

July 3, 2025
Only the Lackeys Are Left
Dear Editors,

As Trump rewards loyalty, so he punishes perceived disloyalty. Trump just threatened North Carolina Republican senator Thom Tillis with a Trump orchestrated primary challenge. Tillis's crime? Demonstrating some independent thought.

Tillis voted against Trump's "Big, Beautiful, Bill." Tillis then immediately announced he would not seek reelection, following the path set by many Republicans (Adam Kinzinger, as one example) who opposed Trump, then left the party, succumbing to his harassment and intimidation. Tillis and others leaving is understandable—who would want to put up with Trump's public calumny and then likely lose your seat? (Kudos to Elizabeth Cheney for at least trying.) However, it leaves the Senate and House Republicans with a carefully curated collection of Trump lackeys.

Their unmitigated devotion seems to have no limits or shame. For example, House Speaker Mike Johnson said, "Do not doubt, do not second guess and don't ever challenge the president of the United States, Donald Trump," and long-time U.S. senator Lindsey Graham said, "I don't mind what Trump does, because I trust Trump."

It is not just the House and Senate. Today, Treasury secretary Scott Bessent said that if he replaces Federal Reserve chair Jerome Powell, who Trump has threatened to fire, even though he legally cannot, "I will do what the president wants."

All of this serves the same purpose—increasing Trump's power as he proceeds with his war on democracy.

———————————

July 11, 2025
Trump as the Anti-Lincoln
Dear Editors,

President Trump's administrator of the EPA, Lee Zelda, just placed more than 170 EPA employees on leave. Their crime? They put their name on a "document of dissent." Another five hundred or so signed anonymously and around five thousand other doctors and scientists signed a letter of support for the stance taken by the EPA employees, comprising a massive dissent. These concerned folks protested Trump's EPA's "promoting misinformation" and "contradicting the EPA's own scientific assessments on human health risks," staff and research grant slashing, and more.

Zelda's action illustrated two of Trump's highest priorities.

First, his long-standing war on the environment. Trump has called climate change a hoax (sometimes a "Democrat hoax," a la the COVID-19 pandemic), even comically stating that windmills were "killing all the birds" and the whales.

Second, his war on dissent. Trump is ridding his administration of any dissenters, appointing and keeping only loyalists. This has already included the DOJ, the Vaccine Advisory Committee, the acting FEMA director, the Head of the Library of Congress, his National Security Advisor, and the list goes on.

Another Republican president, Abraham Lincoln, did the opposite. As described in Doris Kearns Goodwin's book "A Team of Rivals," Lincoln purposely assembled a cabinet composed of prominent political rivals—William Seward, Salmon Chase, and Edward Bates—in part to acknowledge the importance of opposing views and in part to attempt to unite the nation.

This is one of the many ways that Trump is the anti-Lincoln.

————————

July 14, 2025
The Epstein Files: Looney Tunes
Dear Editors,

The furor over the Epstein files, which may or may not contain names of prominent individuals, who may or may not have consorted with women provided by Epstein, including some under legal age, just reached a fevered hysteria.

This old story resurfaced after Attorney General Pam Bondi's U-turn announcement that the client list she once claimed "is sitting on my desk" actually does not exist. The current director of the FBI, Kash Patel, had also said that "the black book [...] (was) under direct control of the director of the FBI." Bondi's comment elicited a significant backlash from MAGA world, most publicly by Trump confidante Laura Loomer and Elon Musk, and behind closed doors by the deputy director of the FBI, Dan Bongino,

President Trump tried to play peace-maker, though on Bondi's side, telling his angry base and others to move on, no story here, "Epstein is dead," and Bondi is "fantastic." And in typical Trump fashion, he claimed that "the Epstein files were written by Obama, Crooked Hillary, [...]" and asked, "Why didn't these Radical Left Lunatics release the files?"

This is an example of Trump trying to solve a problem of his own making. Trump is the one who spiked interest in these files by making a campaign promise to release them, suggesting there would be ignominious revelations, perhaps with legal jeopardy, about political opponents, maybe even the Clintons! Trump was not the only one. J.D. Vance said in October 2024, "Seriously, we need to release the Epstein list. That is an important thing." Still, Trump is the kingpin and his prompting threw fuel on this MAGA fire.

This serious matter, involving sexual exploitation of underage girls, has taken on theatrical overtones. It became Bondi's "Now you have it, now you don't" versus the righteous indignation of people who may have no idea who is on the list, or even if there is a list. Then throw in Trump accusing Obama and Hillary.

A comic turn might seem odd for a topic of this nature, but [...] just think about the cast of characters.

—Bondi is a Big Lie endorser who said of Trump asking Georgia secretary of state Brad Raffensperger to "find 11,780 votes" to reverse the results of that state's 2020 election, "My understanding is that is not what Trump asked him to do."
—Musk has been ostracized by Trump because "Elon has lost his mind."
—Loomer is a conspiracy-monger who called 9/11 "an inside job" and publicly calls Bondi, "blondi," as if that is funny and/or disparaging.
—Bongino is another conspiracy-monger and Big Lie devotee, whose idea of governance is "The only thing that matters is power. Power. That is all that matters. A system of checks and balances. Ha-ha. That's a good one."

All the people involved are there because of Trump, either via appointment or his public support.

When you surround yourself with loonies, you get looney tunes.

———————

July 23, 2025
Alina Habba: Who's On First?
Dear Editors,

Yesterday, a panel of judges of the U.S. District Court of New Jersey declined to retain Alina Habba as New Jersey's top federal prosecutor. Habba had been appointed by Trump's Attorney General Pam Bondi for an interim term pending Senate confirmation within 120 days. That time lapsed without the Senate acting, which legally allowed the district court to name a replacement.

Habba's main qualification for the position appeared to have been her previous service as Trump's personal lawyer and legal spokesperson, one of four Trump personal attorneys (including Emil Bove, John Sauer, and Todd Blanche) to receive appointments in his administration. Prior to working for Trump, she was a partner in a small, six-person law firm, with zero prosecutorial or criminal law experience. With any other president, there would have been thousands of people appointed to this position before her.

Lest there be any question about the extent of Habba's fealty to Trump, after her appointment she told a conservative podcaster that she "was going to paint New Jersey red," filed charges against Democrat mayor Ray Baraka of Newark and Rep. LaMonica Melver (D-N.J.), and announced investigations into New Jersey's Democratic governor Phil Murphy and attorney general Matt Slatkin, all within her first 120 days.

The district court panel appointed Desiree Leigh Grace to replace Habba. Grace was next in line as Habba's First Assistant U.S. attorney and a nine-year federal prosecutor, including service as acting chief of the office's violent crimes unit and chief of the office's criminal division. She is a registered Republican, which suggests that this was not a politically motivated move; instead, she is simply another Republican, but far more qualified and experienced.

Habba's performance on the job may have influenced the district judges, particularly her prosecution of the Democrat Baraka on a seemingly trivial trespass charge at an immigration detention facility. The charge was dismissed by a magistrate judge who publicly chastised Habba for a "worrisome misstep [...] an apparent rush" and felt the need to remind her that "Your role is not to secure convictions at all costs, nor to satisfy public clamor, nor to advance political agendas [...]. Your allegiance is to the impartial application of the law, to the pursuit of truth and to the upholding of due process for all." How often do we hear that kind of scathing public rebuke of a U.S. attorney?

As night follows day, just hours after Grace's appointment, Trump's mega-loyal attorney general Pam Bondi fired Grace.

This prompted a response from New Jersey Democrat senators Cory Booker and Andy Kim, "Trump's Department of Justice [...] showed disregard for the rule of law [...]. The firing of a career public servant (Grace), lawfully appointed by the court, is another blatant attempt to intimidate anyone that doesn't agree with them and undermine judicial independence." All part of Trump's war on democracy.

Desiree Grace then stated that she is honored to be appointed "on merit" and plans on serving "in accordance with the law [...] having served under both Republican and Democrat administrations and having been promoted four times by both." And this after being fired by Bondi.

Trump responded to that by appointing Habba First Assistant U.S. attorney in New Jersey, which makes her Acting U.S. attorney, since in Trump's view, the lead position was unfilled. Now it appears that New Jersey has two U.S. attorneys!

Who knows what is next in this theater of the absurd?

This is the sort of thing that happens when you appoint unqualified loyalists—in this case, both Habba and Bondi—to positions of authority and power. You get the legal version of Abbott and Costello's "Who's on first?"

———————

August 4, 2025
Trump and Laura Loomer: Like-minded Souls
Dear Editors,

Jen Easterly is a West Point graduate, a Rhodes scholar, and an Afghanistan war veteran who has served America admirably for over 30 years, including as a key aide on President George W. Bush's National Security Council, as well as as a cybersecurity expert under President Biden. Fittingly, she was appointed to a prestigious position as the Robert F. McDermott Distinguished Chair in the Department of Social Sciences at West Point.

That same day, far-right wing activist Laura Loomer criticized Easterly on social media, calling her a Biden-era mole. Then, like a patellar reflex response to Loomer, Army Secretary Daniel Driscoll rescinded Easterly's appointment.

Loomer is unelected, has no political experience, and at 32 years old could be said to have little experience at anything. Worse yet, she has used the hashtag "#proudislamophobe" and posted a clapping hands image above the comment "Over 2,000 Migrants Have Died Crossing the Mediterranean So Far This Year." She has been banned from numerous social media platforms. Let us just say that ordinarily this is not a person you would have within a million miles of the occupant of the Oval Office.

Loomer is not a Trump appointee, but she has similar power. She has Trump's ear. And she would not be doing what she is doing without his approval. So let us call her an unofficial appointee.

She is widely "credited" with instigating multiple firings in the Trump administration, including NSA director general Timothy Waugh and his deputy Wendy Noble. Also on her list is Vinay Prasad, the government's top vaccine regulator, Federal Prosecutor Maurene Comey, and six National Security Council officials fired immediately after Loomer informed Trump that those people were disloyal. And now Jen Easterly.

One might wonder, how does someone like this get to be so powerful, or even get an iota of power? But I can see why Trump embraces Loomer—she seems like Trump writ small. She oozes self-confidence, she sees conspiracies and enemies everywhere, and she lashes out aggressively at anyone or anything that she disapproves of. She is completely unfiltered, without recriminations, and without empathy.

She is an unofficial, shadow appointee only because she is a like-minded soul.

————————

August 13, 2025
Trump Replaces the Head of the Bureau of Labor Statistics
(Published in the *Chicago Tribune*)
Dear Editors,

President Donald Trump named Heritage Foundation economist E.J. Antoni as head of the Bureau of Labor Statistics, replacing Erika McEntarfer, whose last jobs report was unfavorable to Trump and got her fired.

The only surprising thing about this was the immediate panning of the appointment by a number of conservative economists on the basis that Antoni was not a competent economist, that he would be in over his head in this position.

Interesting, but beside the point. Antoni was not appointed for his economic credentials.

The real reason was noted by other—again, conservative—economists. For example, Stan Verger, a senior fellow at the conservative American Enterprise Institute, stated that Antoni's work at the Heritage has included errors that "bias his findings in the same partisan direction." Dave Hebert, an economist at the American Institute for Economic Research, stated that "I've been on several programs with him and have been impressed by [...] the speed with which he's gone MAGA." Economist Justin Wolfers said that Antoni is a "1200%, 1300%, maybe 1400% in-the-tank Trumper."

If Antoni is confirmed by the Senate, the analysis of him by conservative economists and the history of Trump appointees tells us that the next jobs report will show a marked improvement in August, and the July report will be revised from negative to positive.

That is the point of his nomination.

CHAPTER 9

THE BIG, BAD, BILL

February 26, 2025
The Opposite of Robin Hood
(Published in the *New York Times*)
Dear Editors,

All major religions—and moral tales of every sort—teach that those who can help others in need should. It's a basic tenet of a good and decent life.

President Trump and his Republican supporters are attempting the opposite. Their primary goal is to give money mostly to the wealthy—with an expected $4.5 trillion in tax cuts. To help finance that, they plan to take money from people far less well-off—by cutting Medicaid, for example, and other services that support those in need.

The attempts to rationalize this by suggesting that states will assume the burdens of payment are flawed. There is a reason the federal government has always borne a huge share of Medicaid costs: most states don't have the money to do so, and they still don't.

President Trump's plan could be summarized: Take from the poor and give to the rich.

I would never have thought so many people would actually support that.

————————

May 15, 2025
Josh Hawley: The GOP Plan Is Immoral (Josh Hawley!!)
Dear Editors,

Kudos to Josh Hawley, the Republican senator from Missouri, for calling the House Republicans' plan to "slash health insurance for the working poor […] morally wrong." The plan violates the biblical maxim that those who can should help those in need. It actually does essentially the opposite: takes from the needy via Medicaid cuts and gives to the more well-off via tax cuts.

Normally, one would look at the 8.6 million Americans projected to lose their health insurance if the House plan is passed, and think, no way, we can't do that to those poor folks, we are supposed to be serving people, not hurting them.

Let's hope that Republican senators follow Mr. Hawley's lead and quash this self-interested, immoral, empathy-less plan.

———————

May 17, 2025
GOP Medicaid Plan: "Cruel and Pointless"
Dear Editors,

In a May 14 *New York Times* op-ed, RFK Jr., Mehmet Oz, Brooke Rollins, and Scott Turner presented what seemed like a sensible plan: "If You Want Welfare and Can Work, You Must." Hard to imagine that anyone believes that people who can work should be allowed to sit at home and accept largesse from those who are working.

However, the following day, Matt Bruenig, in "Medicaid Work Requirements Are Cruel and Pointless," argued that the Medicaid work requirement plan is merely "abstract moral theorizing." Bruenig states that RFK Jr. et al.'s concern actually applies to only 3 percent of people receiving Medicaid benefits. Furthermore, while RFK Jr. et al.'s core theme is that nonworkers receiving Medicaid should be blamed for their unemployment, the reality is that many or most of them have no working options, and as the Trump administration has recently reduced employment rolls by hundreds of thousands of people, with more job losses planned, it is hard to imagine a more inopportune time to be castigating people for not finding employment. In the current milieu, that comes across as name-calling.

Most importantly, this non-solution comes with a huge price, a fatal flaw: the loss of health insurance. Even if you insist that there are lazy folks worthy of blame, the punishment here—loss of health care leading to unnecessary illness and even premature death—is exponentially too severe for the alleged crime. Most of us, and people around the world, believe that health care is a basic right, not conditioned on employment and related moral judgments.

With that understood, the Medicaid work requirement does indeed seem like good "abstract moral theorizing," but lacking when applied to real life. Real life makes better public policy than theory alone.

———————

June 19, 2025
More on Trump Takes From the Poor and Gives to the Rich
Dear Editors,

Apparently, Republican senators are now realizing that Medicaid cuts that cause the closing of rural hospitals are not a good idea.

Thus, Maine governor Susan Collins and others are demanding "provider relief funds" to keep these hospitals open. However, this only addresses the lesser problem. It is generally understood that the "Big, Beautiful Bill" will cause around 10 million people to lose Medicaid, and that holds whether rural hospitals stay open or not. Many of those people will have a nearby open rural hospital they cannot be treated at due to loss of insurance.

This focus on rural hospitals also deflects attention from the bigger picture, which is that the cuts in benefits to the poor are in the same bill that rewards the rich with tax cuts. It is hard for many of us, especially those who provide medical care to the poor, to understand that, as it runs counter to much of what we have learned in life.

———————

June 30, 2025
Trump Posing as Bill Clinton
Dear Editors,

It looks like the "Big Beautiful Bill" is on its way to being the law of the land, now that Lisa Murkowski and Josh Hawley reversed their fervent opposition to Medicaid cuts and loss of funding to rural hospitals. I wonder what is in it for poor and even middle-class people and why they are not rising up in opposition? Polls show that more Americans are against this plan than for it, but it is a rather quiet majority.

The most obvious problem is the cutting in funding to the poor. Recent estimates are that 11.9 million people will lose Medicaid (with some predicted to die as a result) and nutritional assistance will be cut back by around 300 billion dollars (some children will go hungry).

The best argument to justify that is that the national debt is careening out of control with dire prospects ahead for the economic future of our country. Thus, bitter pills need to be swallowed. But since the bill increases spending toward Trump-favored initiatives—specifically the military and the border—and cuts taxes (mostly for the wealthy), the bill is predicted by independent experts to increase the debt by almost $4.0 trillion. That is, many Republican congressmen and senators—like Trump—campaigned on reducing government spending and then immediately voted for the biggest debt increase in history.

In the wake of increasing the debt, Trump cannot argue bitter pill/must reduce the debt, other than to implausibly claim that all the experts are wrong in their predictions.

Basically, he resorts to the old-fashioned Republican fabrication that raising taxes on the rich will lead to an increase in the gross national product (GNP), the debt will decrease, and that and other related economic benefits will accrue to all Americans. That is definitely not the track record of the history of these tax cuts—we have a ton of historical data on changes in tax rates and GNP, poverty rates, and other economic markers. Trump would have you think there has been direct linear relationships between taxes paid by the wealthy and GNP, poverty, and other economic markers, but the reality is that it's more a scattergram, sometimes even in favor of tax increases.

Trump ignores that 10 of the 12 recessions we have had in the United States since the second World War occurred during Republican presidencies.

Trump also constantly reminds people that in his first term, we had "the greatest economy in history" and that he and his tax cuts were responsible.

That claim is dubious. Context is key. It is true that our economy did very well in Trump's first term, with pretty much every major economic indicator showing continued improvement. However, the same can be said for the previous eight Obama years, which had the huge challenge of raising the economy up from the near-dead state that he inherited. Importantly, there seems to be no significant change in the slopes of any basic significant economic indicator after Trump succeeded Obama. Things simply continued to improve at roughly the same rate. That suggests the credit Trump deserves is not for creating the greatest economy ever, but for not messing up the continually improving economy he inherited.

Unfortunately, even with the continued overall improvement and with his tax cuts, the debt soared during Trump's administration—around $7.8 trillion dollars, far more than in Biden's administration—so much so that some called Trump the "King of Debt." That is consistent with his personal history of accumulating so much debt that he declared bankruptcy at least four times.

It actually was in Bill Clinton's tenure—with increased taxes on the rich—that the federal government budget went from a deficit to a surplus and the national debt decreased for the only time in the last 50+ years.

When Trump brags about his economic accomplishments, it seems like he is posing as Bill Clinton.

————————

July 10, 2025
How to Improve the Big, Beautiful, Bill. Why Didn't They?
Dear Editors,

Several Republican senators at first expressed grave concerns over the Big and Beautiful Bill's slashing of funds for health care for the poor and food for children. They eventually voted for it after getting small, face-saving concessions to mitigate the pain in their own states. That was not a principled stand, as they allowed features of the Bill that they considered unacceptable for their own constituents to apply to Americans in all other states.

Concerned Republicans could have and should have taken a more principled stand.

They should have held to their belief that the $1 trillion combined Medicaid and SNAP cuts were unacceptable and had to be eliminated from the bill. Then, in order not to increase the national debt with the restoration of those funds, they should have sought equivalent cuts elsewhere. That actually would have been easy.

Here is how: Roughly $200 billion of new funds are allocated to the southern border to battle illegal immigration. This is a battle President Trump has declared he has already won. Illegal crossings have significantly decreased and deportations have significantly increased. Hard to imagine a real need to pour more money into an already successful project. Hard to imagine that it is more important than health care and food for children.

Presumably, other cuts were also possible. If not, Republicans could have decreased the $4.5 trillion tax cuts to $3.7 trillion. Added to the $200 billion originally intended for the border, that would fully restore the Medicaid and SNAP funds. There is nothing sacrosanct about $4.5 trillion. $3.7 trillion in tax cuts is still a huge number, easily enough for Republicans to claim success and fealty to their platform. Why would any Republicans argue with $3.7 trillion in tax cuts?

The Republicans could easily have provided for the poor and the young, and still provided large tax cuts. Win-win-win.

So why didn't they?

CHAPTER 10

TRUMP'S INVOLVEMENTS IN FOREIGN WARS

February 20, 2025
Trump's Solution for Gaza: A True Horror Show
Dear Editors,

New York Times writer Bret Stephens's concluding sentence, "This horror show of Hamas must end now" is starkly compelling. However, he pays short shrift to Donald Trump's proposed solution: The end not only of Hamas, but the end of Gaza as a home for native Palestinians, the eventual goal being a Trump real estate project dominating the coast and further enriching the Trump Organization. The latter point alone should be met with appropriate condemnation.

Ethnic cleansing is a "horror show" of its own.

——————————

February 21, 2025
Zelensky Does Have Cards to Play
Dear Editors,

President Trump stated that President Zelensky should not be allowed at peace negotiations because "he has no cards." Aside from the bizarre suggestion of excluding one party of a dispute from negotiations, Zelensky actually has a very powerful card, a card that is based on concepts that President Trump, alone among the leaders of the Western Democratic world, cannot understand or recognize. Zelensky's card is the support of the Western world with its commitment to justice, morality, the rule of law, the rights of sovereign countries, the resistance to heinous acts of war, and the support of allies in times of trouble. Plus, awareness of the historical lessons about the calamity of appeasement to tyrants and dictators.

————————

March 4, 2025
From the Grave, Maimonides Chastises Trump
(Published in the *Chicago Sun Times*)
Dear Editors,

President Donald Trump and Vice President J. D. Vance recently demanded a "thank you" from Ukrainian president Volodymyr Zelensky to acknowledge the United States' support of Ukraine, which they suggested was charity. The "thank you" demand was obviously for the sole benefit of Trump's ego.

To paraphrase the great Jewish scholar Maimonides's twelfth-century classic "Eight Rules of Charity," a charitable act is diminished to the extent that the donor benefits. Thus, Trump's and Vance's demand unwittingly diminished their own charitable efforts.

"Thank you," of course, is a nice gesture, but no one with a true sense of charity demands a "thank you."

Furthermore, as Trump and Vance seemed to demand that the recipient metaphorically kneel in obeisance, Maimonides probably would have taught that this was an exercise in power and self-aggrandizement, and not charity at all.

————————

June 18, 2025
Trump Deals With the Iran Crisis that He Created
Dear Editors,

As we await President Trump's momentous decision about whether the United States should join Israel in attacking Iran, or whether he can negotiate a last-minute treaty, several questions seem relevant:

1) To what extent is President Trump responsible for this? After all, we had a treaty with Iran that limited their nuclear capabilities, and he ripped it up. Were the current dire straits predictable, in other words, just a matter of time, when he ended the previous treaty?
2) What possible reasonable reason could there have been for him to end a nuclear-limiting treaty? For sure, many on the right criticized the treaty at the time, but if that criticism had merit, why wouldn't one seek to improve the treaty rather than to abruptly end it?
3) How much of Trump ending the treaty was simply because it was Obama's treaty? Did ending the treaty simply serve his vindictiveness, self-interest, and self-image? Was there ever a careful consideration of the issues solely informed by concern for the well-being of American and the entire world?

———————

July 16, 2025
Trump: The Only One Not to Know (about Putin)
Dear Editors,

Yesterday, President Trump threatened Russia with more tariffs and promised more weapons for Ukraine. In explanation, he cited President Putin's duplicity, "My conversations with him are very pleasant, and then the missiles go off at night. It just keeps going on and on."

Famously, seven years ago to the day—July 16, 2018—in reference to Russian interference in our 2016 presidential election, Trump sided with Putin over his own intelligence community, saying, "I have President Putin. He just said it's not Russia. I will say this. I don't see any reason why it would be."

Assuming that yesterday's comment reflected an actual revelation, rather than just a meaningless ad lib, it is reassuring that Trump finally figured out that Putin has been playing him all along. However, it is unsettling to think that it took Trump seven years to see what was readily apparent to everyone else.

Trump was the only one not to know.

———————

July 21, 2025
Bombing Iran: The Little Lie
Dear Editors,

It is now one month since President Trump's military strike on Iran and his immediate claim that the United States "completely destroyed, totally obliterated" Iran's three nuclear sites and that Iran's nuclear capabilities were set back "decades."

That was not a lie, because Trump did not know it to be false at the time. However, it could be said to be dishonest in that Trump presented it with certainty, when it was obviously too early to be supported by actual evidence.

A president less driven by self-aggrandizement and braggadocio might have said, "The mission was a success, we destroyed much of Iran's nuclear capacity and significantly set back their time table to produce a nuclear bomb. Exactly how much we destroyed and how much we set back their enrichment capabilities will be determined by assessments over the next few weeks."

As it turned out, American intelligence, Israeli intelligence, and the International Atomic Energy Agency have all—a consensus of experts—denied Trump's grandiose claim.

Two of Iran's three enrichment sites appear to have been less damaged, at least one of which reportedly has enriched uranium, and the recent estimates of how far Iran's nuclear capability has been pushed back range from several months to a couple of years. Still, that is an excellent result—Iran's nuclear capabilities were diminished, we demonstrated that we could do this easily and, if needed, probably again in the future. That might serve as a useful deterrent going forward.

However, Trump and his representatives are sticking with "completely destroyed, totally obliterated." The contrary evidence cited is variably attributed to "the Fake News Media" and/or to "experts are not experts, we are the experts."

Thus, it appears that Trump's initial dishonesty has evolved into a sustained lie. By now he knows that his initial claim was exaggerated and has been refuted by the actual evidence, and yet he repeats it anyway. This is far short of the Big

Lie which roiled the country and birthed a mob's attempt to thwart democracy by allowing the loser of the election to be declared the winner. In comparison, this might be called The Little Lie.

All of this reminds us that almost nothing Trump says in the political arena can be taken at face value.

When Trump speaks, we need to ask: What size lie is this?

————————

August 2, 2025
Trump Loves His Strong Men, but They Play Him
Dear Editors,

President Trump recently expressed frustration with President Putin, realizing that Putin was not interested in peace with Ukraine, other than totally on his terms, and had been stringing Trump along with false promises, deceptions, and the like. In slang terms, Putin has been playing Trump.

Current reporting from Israel now suggests that Trump's other buddy, Israeli prime minister Bibi Netanyahu, is also playing Trump, but in this case, Trump remains unaware. This is difficult to write because Hamas is so evil, their October 7 attack so savage, and I am a long-time supporter of Israel. All that aside, Netanyahu seems like Putin, interested in peace only on his own terms, if at all, which led to the recent mass starvation in Gaza. That is a horrific story on its own, but for present purposes, the point is about Trump's role in this.

Specifically, Israel's daily newspaper *Haaretz* reports that Netanyahu broke a cease-fire with Hamas in March for personal political reasons, imposed new conditions of surrender on Hamas, and then resumed the war. His cover story, which apparently Trump approved, was that harsher military blows on Hamas and more hardships on Gazan civilians would finally incite an uprising, or bring Hamas to its knees and free the remaining hostages. Instead, no more hostages have been released, thousands more Palestinian civilians have been killed, and the world has looked on in horror at the humanitarian disaster that unfolded one tragic day at a time. All the while, Trump stood by.

Trump has supported Netanyahu throughout, and his support may have been a requisite for Netanyahu to break the cease-fire and proceed in barbaric fashion.

Will Trump ever realize that Putin was not the only one to have played him?

————————

August 16, 2025
Ninety-Nine Percent Bully, One Percent Lapdog
Dear Editors,

The summit between President Trump and President Putin concerning the Russia-Ukrainian war just ended.

Trump entered the meeting having recently criticized Putin for duplicity and threatening "severe consequences," including major economic sanctions if Putin did not agree by Friday to "stop the killing" with a cease-fire. He stressed that the onus was on Putin to do so. Trump also endorsed, after a meeting earlier this week with European powers, their long-held position that Ukraine would not cede any of its sovereign territory to Russia under any circumstances.

Trump left the Summit stating that there would be no cease-fire, no immediate ending to the killings, no new deadline, no consequences to Putin, and that Ukraine would have to cede land (including some areas not even occupied by Russia) in order to reach a peace agreement. Additionally, he proclaimed that the onus was on President Zelensky to accept Putin's conditions, and on European nations to get more involved, meaning pressure Zelensky to capitulate.

In other words, Trump did a U-turn on every issue at hand, embracing Putin's stance on everything important.

This complete capitulation to Putin made the famous Muhammad Ali first-round knockout of Sonny Liston seem like a competitive fight. In an iconic image, Ali stood over the fallen Liston, taunting him, "Get up and fight, you coward." There is no reason to think Putin taunted Trump afterwards, but he very likely laughed all the way home from Alaska.

I have two questions:

First, what could Putin possibly have said to get Trump to reverse himself on every issue? How could anyone be that compelling? Oh to have been a fly on that wall!

Second, more broadly, Trump is a bully to the rest of the world. He operates by "do what I say, or I will apply a heavy tariff." How can an intransigent, intrinsic bully turn into a lapdog in the face of one person, and one person only? It seems so odd: 99 percent bully, 1 percent lapdog.

August 20, 2025
The Art of the Deal. By Vladimir Putin
Dear Editors,

Back-to-back meetings between President Trump and President Putin, and then with Trump, President Zelensky, and seven European leaders ended without a deal to end the Russia-Ukraine war. Almost immediately, hostilities resumed as Putin re-attacked Ukraine with drones and missiles, leaving more than 1,400 residences and more than 100 businesses without power.

If these meetings were akin to a boxing match, Putin would be declared the winner by unanimous decision. Putin coerced Trump to back off on every position that Trump had previously supported, including his prior insistence on either an immediate cease-fire or sanctions on Russia. We now have no cease-fire and no sanctions.

Furthermore, the meetings ended without any concrete plans going forward. Or with Putin showing any inclination to actually reach a deal. Quite the opposite, he maintained his steadfast claims on Ukrainian land, which seems to be his particular line in the sand.

Putin drags his feet because he is gaining leverage as time goes by. The battle on the ground has tilted in his favor. He knows that Trump admires him and considers Putin an interlocutor with reasonable demands, not a warmonger to be feared. The need for seven European leaders at the second meeting to support Zelensky speaks volumes to the widespread belief that Trump favors Putin.

Putin also knows that Trump is obsessed with winning a Nobel Peace Prize. In Trump's pursuit of the Prize, it is likely that as the war drags on, he will get increasingly frustrated with Zelensky and his supporters, continue to tilt in Putin's direction, and eventually coerce Zelensky to sign almost any peace treaty, even if one-sided in Russia's favor.

Zelensky and European leaders will resist, but they have little sway without Trump's firm support and little ability to resist Trump's coercion.

From the Russian point of view, Putin is playing this masterfully, with Trump as his marionette.

The "Art of the Deal" apparently was written by Putin, not Trump.

CHAPTER 11

TRUMP'S MENTATION

February 23, 2025
The Dangerous Case of Donald Trump
Dear Editors,

Kimberly Clausing's article "The Real Reason Trump Pushes Tariffs" in the *New York Times* provides a rational and erudite discussion of President Trump's thinking. Very informative, but it assumes that Trump's thinking is rational and that he actually gave thought to the details. An alternate explanation is that it is not rational. That is, he does things like this because he can and because it makes him look and feel all-powerful.

The same could be, and has been, said about his territorial aspirations (Greenland, Canada, Gaza), his unprecedented attempted expansion of the powers of the presidency, his hyperbolic disdain for anyone who opposes him, and much of his commentary, including that so many things are rigged or faked. His governing dynamic seems to be that as president of the United States, he can do whatever he pleases.

It may have been best exemplified in his first term in his stance on masking to prevent illness from COVID-19. Rather than follow scientific and epidemiological evidence and the advice of experts, Trump ignored all that, saying, "Can you imagine how weak I'd look wearing a mask?" and then advising against mask use. This fueled similar mask disdain in many of his followers, many of whom suffered the ravages of COVID-19 as a result.

Trump's propensity for irrational thinking is discussed in "The Dangerous Case of Donald Trump: 27 Psychiatrists and Mental Health Experts Assess a President" by Bandy X. Lee. At a minimum, this analysis from experts should give pause for thought for those who evaluate Trump's machinations as if they are rational.

———————

March 11, 2025
Trump Defies John Lennon
Dear Editors,

John Lennon once said that "Reality leaves a lot to the imagination," reflecting standard thinking that we can imagine much more than what can actually take place.

Recent events inverted this historical adage. Reality has transcended anything our imagination could ever evoke.

For example, no one could have imagined that a U.S. president would ally with Russia against a Western democracy, but President Trump paused military aid and the flow of intelligence information to Ukraine, blamed Ukraine for starting the war, denied that President Putin was responsible, and is coercing Ukraine into accepting a peace treaty entirely on Russian terms, rewarding Putin's criminal invasion with land annexation.

Nor could one have imagined that an anti-vaccine, anti-science, irrational thinker like RFK Jr. could be confirmed as secretary of Health and Human Services in a modern society. Yet he was, and recently he touted ineffectual Vitamin A and cod liver oil treatments for a measles outbreak while largely keeping quiet about the vaccine that actually prevents the disease.

Nor that Elon Musk, who believes that Social Security is "the biggest Ponzi scheme of all time" and that "the fundamental weakness of Western civilization is empathy," would be placed in a position of power.

Lennon would surely have been surprised at how modern events have exposed the limits of our imagination.

———————

May 21, 2025
Trump, Biden's Cancer, and Lack of Human Decency
Dear Editors,

President Trump, his son, and various others have suggested that Joe Biden and those around him have long known of and hidden his prostate cancer diagnosis.

Medically speaking, prostate cancer screening is not routinely recommended for those over 70 years old. Even if Mr. Biden had a PSA test last year, his particularly aggressive form of prostate cancer could easily have developed since then. So, absent actual details, there is no valid reason for Mr. Trump's speculation.

From a broader perspective of human decency, Mr. Trump's suggestion is awful. Imagine using another human being's life-threatening health condition to criticize that person solely for your own political enhancement. I understand that politics is commonly dog-eat-dog, but this seems to reach new depths.

————————

June 1, 2025
Trump's Craziness Is Craziness, Not Reason in Disguise
Dear Editors,

Ross Douhat (*New York Times* op-ed) argues in "A President Often Willing To Swerve Or Backpedal" that President Trump's apparent craziness is part of a calculated strategy, that his extremism is provisional and his "re-calibrations" ultimately yield benefits without harms.

This Pollyanna idea is completely rebutted by Nicholas Kristof's "The Human Toll of Trump's Aid Cuts," which cites the enormous toll of the dismantling of USAID and the loss of health care abroad: "The only debate is whether to measure the dead in the thousands, tens of thousands or hundreds of thousands" (and still mounting).

Furthermore, hundreds of thousands of jobs were lost to the craziness of DOGE, which even Elon Musk admitted saved trivial money. Musk's departure and a re-calibration are no solace to those many newly unemployed who are struggling to support themselves and their families.

The downsizing or elimination of various Federal departments deprived many of the needy of necessary services. Those poor folks are also suffering.

The proposed cuts to Medicaid are predicted to lead to eight-plus million people losing their health insurance, with unnecessary illnesses and even deaths certain to follow.

There are more examples yet.

Mr. Douhat's assertion that Trump's outré policies are commonly reversed without harm to others simply ignores the vast suffering his policies have caused many Americans. That is not reason in disguise.

———————

June 25, 2025
Was the Bombing of Iran a Rational Choice or an Ego Stroke?
Dear Editors,

In his first term, President Trump tore up, without replacement, a previous agreement (the JCPOA) with Iran that effectively limited their nuclear capabilities. Thus, Trump's recent bombings addressed a problem—per his own telling, a crisis—of his own unnecessary making.

The difference in Trump's approach seems striking and needs explanation. In the first instance, tearing up the treaty without replacing it, he seemed unconcerned with Iran's nuclear capabilities. Now, years later, he took the exact opposite approach: an extremely aggressive, hyper-concerned, crisis-style response. Why the dramatic discrepancy? Did the situation change that radically?

Hopefully, both cases reflected careful consideration of intelligence information, consultation with experts in the area, evaluation of risks and benefits, and the sorts of cautious and meticulous evaluation we expect of our leaders when they make momentous decisions.

On the other hand, there is reason to be concerned about a scary alternative, that Trump did little to none of the above and made seemingly opposing decisions based on the common thread of self-interest. Perhaps, in the first case, vindictiveness and power—"this was Obama's treaty, have to get rid of it [...] I can undo whatever Obama did, I am in charge now." And more recently, "look how fantastic how military is, look how powerful I am, Iran will come to heel."

If that is the case, then even if the Iran bombing turns out to be a wonderful thing, it will have been for the wrong reasons. The success will be a cause for great cheer, but the thinking process will be a cause of great alarm for what lies ahead.

————————

July 24, 2025
Trump's Weird Obama Fixation Re-surfaces
Dear Editors,

Which of the following is the most preposterous?

—The Earth is flat.
—The moon landing was a hoax.
—9/11 was an inside job.
—Jews shot lasers from outer space to start California wildfires.
—Haitians ate cats and dogs in Ohio.

Or, the most recent candidates, uttered on consecutive days by President Trump:

—President Barack Obama created the Epstein files.
—Obama engineered the fake story that Russians interfered with the 2016 election.

Trump's latest slurs continue his long-time odd fixation with Obama. This goes back to the evidence-less birther conspiracy, which he continued to espouse long after it had been thoroughly debunked. It also seemed to manifest in attempts to reverse many of Obama's signature accomplishments including, unsuccessfully, the Affordable Care Act and, successfully, the withdrawals from the climate change Paris Agreement and the nuclear weapons Iran Agreement. Trump has also issued a series of childish, unprovoked insults at Obama over the years, including "he's a jerk," "he's a divider," "he's a bad speaker," and often referred to Obama by his middle name Hussein, oddly intended as an insult.

The latest Trump Obama-directed barbs compete for "craziest ideas" ever because they require preposterous underpinnings.

Trump's theory on the Epstein files posits that 10 years ago, in cahoots with James Comey and others in the Republican-led FBI, Obama came up with the idea to fabricate these files for release a decade later upon demand by the MAGA base and far-right wing commentators, but not to use the files in the 2016, 2020, or 2024 elections. Enough said.

The second part suggests that Attorney General Pam Bondi is going to find evidence nine years later—the Justice Department just announced a "Strike Force"—that Obama, as Trump said, committed treason, punishable by death, by leading an effort to falsely tie Trump to Russian interference in the 2016 election.

That would mean that a horde of Republican investigators covered up Obama's treason for years, with Trump keeping his own silence on this matter up until now.

The ~400 page Mueller (a Republican) Report documented extensive Russian interference without citing any misdeed by Obama. Then, in 2020, the Republican-led Senate Intelligence Committee, headed by Trump's current Secretary of State Republican Marco Rubio, released a nearly 1,000 page report concluding that Russia did interfere in the election—"We found irrefutable evidence of Russian meddling"—and made no incriminating mention of Obama.

And the subsequent Republican Durham Report landed with a thud, a single conviction (with no jail time) of someone no one ever heard of, for altering an email, and no evidence against Obama.

Does anyone believe that all those Republicans spent all that time and effort hiding Obama's treason?

Or is it obvious that this is standard Trump procedure? When things are going bad, distract.

President Trump has not done so well recently. His name is reportedly in the sex offender Epstein files, which disturbs Trump, even if Trump committed no crime. He has been alleged by the *Wall Street Journal* to have sent a risqué birthday card to Epstein, and his approval ratings declined to a second term low of 37 percent in the latest Gallup poll. The latter likely reflects increasing disenchantment with his cruel, excessive deportation policy, his on again-off again tariffs, his Big, Bad, Bill with all its obvious deficiencies, his relentless attacks on foes home and abroad, and his "a new crazy crisis every day" style.

No matter how absurd, it seems like Obama is Trump's go-to guy for distraction.

———————

August 1, 2025
The July Jobs Report: From One "Rigged" Point to Another
Dear Editors,

A very poor jobs report was released yesterday revealing that the United States added only 73,000 jobs in July, well below expectations. President Trump responded—you can't make this up!—by calling it "rigged [...] in order to make ME look bad [...] the numbers were phony" and firing the Bureau of Labor Statistics commissioner, Erica McEntarfer. McEntarfer had been confirmed by the Senate 86-8 in 2024, with the "yea" votes including J. D. Vance, Marco Rubio, and a large number of other Republicans. "Shooting the messenger" is widely understood as folly.

This was both bizarre and not surprising at all.

It was bizarre, as many in the field pointed out, because scores, some said hundreds, of employees are involved in the jobs report and "rigging" would require a covert conspiracy of epic proportions, of apolitical civil servants risking their careers for a [...] single jobs report?

Also bizarre that senior Trump officials responsible for running our economy went along with this comic Trump ploy, apparently too frightened and cowardly to speak up.

It was not surprising because you can draw a direct line between "they rigged my inauguration photo" to "they rigged the 2020 Election" to "they rigged the July jobs report," with a large number of additional "data points" on the line.[1]

In the gentlest view of a thinking process that yields repetitive "rigging" conspiracies, one wonders how anyone can trust anything Trump says. It is not just the proverbial "cockroach in the bowl of spaghetti"; it is a bowl of spaghetti riddled with cockroaches.

———————

August 12, 2025
Trump's Alternative Facts: Still a Pig
Dear Editors,

In January 2017, at the beginning of President Trump's first term, presidential Counselor Kellyanne Conway introduced the term "alternative facts" to describe President Trump's and spokesman Sean Spicer's provably false statements about inauguration crowd sizes. Almost everyone scoffed at her at the time—what a crazy comment! But it turned out that she was prescient, a seeress, in predicting that this would be Trump's modus operandi as president. She knew that he would routinely look the country in the eye and say things that were false, knowing full well that what he was saying was false, and yet proceeding anyway as if his words were true.

For example, and just recently:

—Trump stated that President Obama created the Epstein files for use against a then New York businessman a decade later.
—He stated that the latest job report was "rigged" and that job creation had actually increased.

---

1 Just two weeks later, Trump added another data point to his conspiracy line, "The D.C. crime data are rigged."

—He sent the National Guard into D.C. and took control of the police force, describing "bloodthirsty criminals, roving mobs of wild youth, drugged-out maniacs [...]" in a city where violent crime has decreased to a 30-year low.
—He threatened that Chicago, where "crime is out of control," would be his next federal takeover target. Chicago also had a historic drop in violent crime this year—a 30 to 40 percent decline in shootings and homicides—continuing a four-year favorable trend.
—On the eve of a summit with President Putin, he again blamed President Zelensky for Putin's invasion.

Describing bold-faced lies as "alternative facts" recalls the adage, "you can put lipstick on a pig, but it is still a pig."

————————

August 28, 2025
Trump's Quest for the Nobel Peace Prize Is Ignoble
Dear Editors,

Once or twice a week now, President Trump, or one of his acolytes, advocates publicly for Trump to receive the Nobel Peace Prize, citing his success in ending six or, sometimes, seven wars.

There are several disturbing aspects to this.

First, it appears that Trump's claim is false. Several of the conflicts are ongoing, and several others ended with minimal input on his part. And the two conflicts with the most widespread ramifications—in Ukraine and in Gaza—both rage on, with Trump's efforts having had no significant benefit as yet.

Trump's campaign for the Prize is itself evidence that he has over-hyped or even fabricated his claims. Nobel Prize–deserving acts speak for themselves. If you need to tout them, they are not likely worthy of the Prize. No one who actually deserves the Nobel Prize ever publicly campaigns for it. Trump does not realize that his public campaign to win the Prize is self-disqualifying.

Yet this behavior is not at all surprising. Trump's fixation on receiving this award reflects his insatiable need to be told how magnificent he is. Nothing could be more gratifying to someone so ego-fragile than receiving such a prestigious award, announced with fanfare to the entire world.

We have seen this many times from Trump. For example, at White House staff meetings that start by going around the table, one attendee after another, praising the president. Only after that do they get down to business. And we hear Republican senators and U.S. representatives publicly laud the great man. This is a standard demand by Trump, and a common response by others having to deal with him.

As a result, the animated TV show "South Park" has a running skit in which leaders of countries around the world stand in line in the White House waiting their turn to give Trump gifts and exaltation. The skit is meant for laughs—and derision—but good satire is rooted in reality.

Sadly, this is not just a benign personality disorder to be scoffed at, or sympathized with, but not warranting concern. Something so fundamental and important to Trump cannot be separated from his decision-making. For example, he placed smaller tariffs on countries whose leaders were more obsequious to him, larger tariffs on those less- or un-flattering. Mayors and governors know that the means to avoid federal takeover of their jurisdiction is to praise Trump; he only invades or threatens cities governed by Trump-averse officials.

Even more importantly, this is playing out publicly with the negotiations to end the Russia-Ukraine war. It started in February when Trump kicked Ukrainian president Zelensky out of the White House for not being properly thankful and laudatory—no fawning, therefore, nothing to talk about; servility first, then peace. Recently, we witnessed in real life what looked like a spoof of the South Park spoof, with seven European leaders at the recent White House summit beginning the meeting by paying homage to Trump, one after the other. That included Zelensky, who had learned his lesson.

Even the heartless warmonger President Putin, a few days earlier at the Alaska Summit with Trump, began the meeting with obsequious fawning, only to return to character later on by restarting the war.

All of these world leaders knew that Trump is influenced by flattery, and acted on that basis. Hard to believe, but Trump's compulsive need for private and public adoration is actually a factor in these peace negotiations.

Trump's Nobel Prize obsession is a variation on that theme.

Nobel Peace Prize winners have always been noble, motivated by doing great deeds, rather than by receiving an award.

Donald Trump seeks the award to satisfy his ego. That is ignoble.

CHAPTER 12

WAR ON SO MANY THINGS

April 27, 2025
The War on Jobs: DOGE Is a Problem, Not a Solution
Dear Editors,

It turns out that the 150 billion dollars that Elon Musk claims he saved in the war on the federal job force will be opposed by a DOGE-induced cost of 135 billion dollars. The actual savings will be about 15 billion dollars, or much less than one percent of the nearly $7 trillion the federal government spent in the 2024 fiscal year. Everyday Americans have derived minimal to no benefit from this.

In stark contrast, perhaps several hundred thousand federal workers lost their jobs. Many of them are now struggling to support themselves and their families, often with no alternate employment in sight. Other people are, or will be, suffering from the loss of needed services, including health care, that these erstwhile workers and their depleted agencies are no longer able to provide.

There has been a lot of pain, and very little gain.

American commentator H. L. Mencken stated that every complex problem has a solution that is simple—and wrong. Those solutions are not solutions; they are new problems.

DOGE is a problem, not a solution.

———————

May 6, 2025
Trump Targets Veterans
Dear Editors,

The indignities and harms of DOGE continue to pile up. In addition to the several hundred thousand people now out of work and many others suffering from the loss of important services, we now learn ("V.A. Staff, Crammed in Offices, Says Patient Privacy is Suffering" *New York Times*, May 6) that psychiatric nurses are treating veterans with mental health conditions in a hallway near a bathroom. Furthermore, that the Trump administration announced plans to eliminate 80,000 Department of Veterans Affairs (VA) jobs. As a result, many clinicians have reported that they plan to start looking for jobs outside the VA system.

Why would anyone treat veterans in this manner?

———————

June 24, 2025
Trump's War Against Science
(Published in the *Chicago Sun Times*)
Dear Editors,

To paraphrase Martin Luther King Jr., "The arc of science is long, but it bends towards progress." However, that was only true before President Donald Trump's reelection. Bizarrely, Trump has effectively declared a war on, of all things, science. For example, he is trying to slash funds for the CDC, NIH, NASA, National Science Foundation, and various university research grants, all of which will have deleterious effects.

He also appointed the anti-vaccine, anti-science RFK Jr. as head of the Department of Health and Human Services. RFK Jr., with Trump's approval, fired the entire vaccine board of the CDC, surely to find replacements specifically chosen to disparage vaccines.

Vaccines are some of the greatest scientific achievements of the last 200-plus years. They have eradicated smallpox, polio, and nearly measles, and are very effective against malaria, shingles, tetanus, hepatitis, COVID-19, to name but a few.

To whatever extent RFK Jr. (with Trump's support) succeeds in his anti-vaccine agenda, some of those diseases will be revitalized in their ability to cause illness and death. Newer viruses that emerge will result in unnecessary damage. We will likely see, once again, a tragic part of the COVID-19 pandemic that practicing physicians and nurses witnessed: people in their deathbeds expressing regrets over having refused a vaccine.

All of this is the exact opposite of "[...] bending towards progress."

Trump's war on science is one of the saddest things I have seen during my 40 years practicing medicine.

———————

June 25, 2025
Trump's War on Transgenders: Ask, Don't Tell
Dear Editors,

My heart goes out to Samantha Williams, her transgender daughter, and the transgender community after the Supreme Court ruled against them. Worse yet, the ruling follows President Trump's executive order, with its too-simplistic decree of two distinct sexes only, and its formal invalidation of an entire community of Americans.

The scientific reality behind sex determination is that it is complicated. There are a number of chromosomal variations that may lead to non-classic phenotypes (outward appearances) including ambiguous genitalia. There are also poorly understood self-perceptions, perhaps with a neurobiologic basis, that affect sexuality. These are people who truly do not fit into the classic male or female categories. Trying to legislate them away is a fool's errand; it doesn't make them disappear, it just gratuitously harms them.

In this sometimes difficult realm, one thing I am sure of is that no one like Trump, who knows nothing about any of this, should be making binding decisions that affect the lives of others. His trans-denying executive order was obviously devoid of empathy, open-mindedness, tolerance, and was not based on scientific knowledge.

Supreme Court Justice Clarence Thomas, for his own purposes, acknowledged the scientific uncertainty of sexual orientation, stating that "In politically contentious debates over matters shrouded in scientific uncertainty, courts should not assume that self-described experts are correct." Actually, there should be no politics in this; it is a medical and scientific matter. It is only political if you make it so by approaching the topic, like Trump and Thomas, with political ideology and self-interest, rather than science. In addition, Thomas's demeaning of "self-described experts" is telling and noxious in several ways. First, it is a childish *ad hominem.* Second, it is dishonest, as he surely knows the "experts" are not "self-described." There is a field of intelligent, respected physicians and scientists who have studied human sexuality for their entire professional careers and actually have advanced our knowledge. Third, it is Trump, Thomas, and their supporters who express their unscientific opinions as dogma, for example, via legislative fiat, as opposed to the professionals in the field, who typically do the opposite, humbly respecting ambiguity and human variation.

As a practicing physician, I long ago learned a broadly applicable, simple guideline for these matters: If you want to know what sex a person is, or how to address them, or about anything related, just ask them. And then listen. They will tell you what you need to know.

Ask, don't tell.

————————

June 26, 2025
War on the IRS: How Is This Going to Help?
Dear Editors,

President Trump has delivered a solid one-two punch to the IRS. The first, a left hook to the jaw, came earlier this year, when he fired 6,700 IRS employees, with many more planned to go. Trump has also proposed a significant cut in IRS funding. The obvious direct result of this will be that there will be fewer audits. More tax cheats will get away with their crimes, and, realizing that, more people will cheat on their taxes.

Thus, an organization whose mission is to collect all money owed will collect less money. This will make our huge national debt even worse. It is hard to even imagine interventions that are more self-defeating.

The nonpartisan Budget Lab at Yale predicts that these changes will lead to nearly $395 billion in forgone revenue over the next 10 years, and if the lack of IRS resources results in increased noncompliance, as expected, the forgone revenue could reach as high as $2.4 trillion over 10 years.

Then came the second punch, this time a right cross, in the form of yesterday's Senate confirmation of Trump's appointee Ken Kies, to lead the Office of Tax Policy. Kies has spent his professional career fighting for tax breaks for businesses and wealthy people. He has also facilitated, as a lobbyist and advisor, tax avoidance strategies used by multinational companies and wealthy Americans, including lobbying in favor of tax havens. Basically, he is an expert in helping people and businesses avoid paying taxes.

How is a person with that skill set and those interests going to help the IRS?

———————————

July 2, 2025
The CFPB Purge: Why Is Trump Protecting Fraud?
Dear Editors,

The Consumer Financial Protection Bureau (CFPB) was one of DOGE's targets. The Trump administration tried to fire about 90 percent of the bureau's staff. That is currently on hold due to lawsuits, but Trump's aim is clear.

The CFPB was meant to oversee our banks and financial services companies, protect consumers, detect fraud, and then provide compensation when appropriate. Over the last 15 years, it has returned approximately $21 billion to defrauded customers, a huge success story. Trump is trying to end this.

Worse yet, under Trump, the CFPB has actually reversed course from its original purpose. In May, it annulled a previous order for Toyota to compensate defrauded customers $48 million. And yesterday, the CFPB dismissed an $80 million refund to servicemen and women who had paid fees illegally charged by the Navy Federal Credit Union.

This begs the question: Why is President Trump supporting business fraud at the expense of American citizens?

———————————

July 8, 2025
The "A" in MAGA Is for America Only
(Published in the *Chicago Tribune*)
Dear Editors,

The U.S. Agency for International Development just formally closed its doors after 60 years of global humanitarian operations. Recently, the noted medical journal *Lancet* published a study indicating that the loss of this funding could lead to 14 million unnecessary deaths by 2030.[1]

How could President Donald Trump do this? Fourteen million dead people! Regarding foreign affairs, the first "A" in MAGA now stands for "only America!"

In that view of the world, deaths in African countries and other poor areas are simply not important. They are not Americans; they are not part of "Make America Great Again." They just do not matter.

Notably, a previous Republican president, George W. Bush, had the opposite view of the world. Many believe that Bush's greatest accomplishment was his PEPFAR program, which financed HIV treatment and relief in 50 countries. PEPFAR reportedly saved around 25 million lives.

Bush responded appropriately to the USAID closing in a message to its now unemployed workers: "You've showed the great strength of America through your work—and that is your good heart. Is it in our national interests that 25 million people who would have died now live? I think it is, and so do you."

Thank goodness for Bush's good heart.

————————

1 Dr. Craig Spencer, professor at Brown University School of Public Health and member of the advisory board of Doctors Without Borders USA, commented that as a result of Trump's global health cutbacks, "Virtually overnight and all around the world, lifesaving care has vanished. HIV medications have become inaccessible for millions, newborn care has halted in many war zones, and communal kitchens feeding Sudanese civilians amid conflict have closed."

July 10, 2025
Shutting Down USAID Is Even Worse for Young Women
Dear Editors,

Many experts in the field, particularly those who have spent their careers providing humanitarian aid in Africa, have decried the deaths the shutting of USAID will certainly cause. But that does not capture all of it.

For example, many poor girls in Africa cannot afford menstrual pads. So, during their periods, they stay home from school, as often as one week every month. This sometimes leads to them dropping out of school at a young age, which leads to, well [...] you get the point.

It gets even worse. The girls often rely on boys with money to pay for sanitary pads. *New York Times* columnist Nicholas Kristof, who regularly reports from Africa, quoted an unnamed girl as saying, "If you give them something, they will give you something in return." We know what that means.

The ending of USAID will worsen this particular indignity.

Kristof discussed the role Western feminism should play in fighting back. I do not see the need to emphasize any niche of dissenters: All people, men and women, should recoil from this story.

———————

July 16, 2025
Trump's War on Canada: Who Picks Fights With Their Friends?
Dear Editors,

President Trump recently increased his tariff on Canada, our neighbor, our great friend, and our ally, to 35 percent. Trump typically cites "the tremendous flow of fentanyl and immigrants across the U.S.-Canada border" as the justification. This is an obvious fabrication—a stalking horse. It is well-documented that the flow of fentanyl and illegal crossings across that border is trivial. Worse yet, the tariff has been accompanied by all sorts of insults flowing north.

Trump seems to forget that Canadians are people. They react to purposeless slights exactly as one would expect. Recent polls show that 59 percent of

Canadians view the United States as their "greatest threat," 72 percent intend to avoid buying U.S.-made products, and 75 percent intend to forgo travel here.

Obviously, the goodwill between these two once-great allies is plummeting. How low will it get? Will it eventually get repaired? What is the point?

Who picks fights with a friend?

———————

July 20, 2025
Trump's War on Rural America
Dear Editors,

One of the oddest things about President Trump's war on the federal workforce, federal programs, and perceived liberal enemies is how disproportionately it harms his rural base. And how little they seem to sense that, or at least to publicly complain.

That is most obvious with the recent Medicaid cuts. Fifty percent of rural children get health care from Medicaid. The cuts are so likely to ravage rural hospitals—even lead to closings—that Republican senator Lisa Murkowski of Alaska and Senator Susan Collins of Maine refused to commit to a "yes" vote until the bill was revised to include a $50 billion rural health care fund. Still, that fund seemed mostly performative, a drop in the bucket, as the cuts to Medicaid funding are approximately $1 trillion.

Fifteen percent of people in small towns and rural areas depend on the federal food assistance program, SNAP, to feed their families. This assistance has been cut by almost $300 billion.

Trump's mass deportation program adversely affects farms, which commonly rely on immigrants for manual labor. This did prompt enough of a backlash from farmers that Trump, if only for a moment, pledged to stop immigration raids on farms, stating "[…] our very aggressive policy on immigration is taking very good, long-time workers away from them, with those jobs being almost impossible to replace." However, following this announcement, the farm raids quickly resumed.

Now we have one more Trump slap in the face to rural America. The recent canceling of $1.1 billion for public broadcasting was based on Trump's view of these stations as "left-wing monstrosities." That overrode, for him and almost all Republican legislators, their beneficial role in rural America, particularly in providing local news and public safety information, including weather alerts. Senator Murkowski cited "the incredible public service these stations provide," including "emergency alerts that save human lives." Colorado senator Michael Bennet noted that "During floods and wildfires, radio is often the only source of information for rural and tribal communities." That is because around 20 percent of households in rural communities do not have internet access. The 10 states with the lowest internet access all have large rural areas, with Montana and Alaska leading with approximately 30 percent of their populations lacking access. These are the areas that will be hardest hit by reducing access to public media.

Will Trump's rural base figure out that MAGA does not seem to include them?

—————————

July 27, 2025
Trump's War on Women in the Military
Dear Editors,

Much could be said about President Trump's sordid history with women—his adultery with a porn star, his sexual assault civil conviction, his many degrading comments, and so on—but let us concentrate on his recent approach to women in the military.

In the decade or so prior to Trump's reelection, the role of women in the U.S. military soared. They now comprise about 16 percent of the total force, with an 18 percent increase in female enlistment in 2024 over the previous year. Further, since the Obama administration, women have not been excluded from any type of combat mission, including Special Operations and elite Marine Corps units. It should come as no surprise that incorporating and encouraging female recruitment in the military has been widely considered to have improved our armed forces.

This notion reversed instantly with Trump's reelection and then his appointment of Pete Hegseth as defense secretary. Hegseth had to defend himself in his confirmation hearings from charges of being antagonistic to women in the military. To win confirmation, by just 51-50, he had to walk back a litany of previous derogatory comments, particularly to win the vote of Senator Joni Ernst (R-Iowa), an army veteran who had commanded troops in Iraq and Kuwait.

Trump began to address his perceived problem of female officers on day one with the firing of Admiral Linda Lee Fagan, Coast Guard commandant, who had served in that role for three years and was the first uniformed woman to lead this military branch. He followed that with an executive order ending diversity programs in the military, suggesting that female promotions had often not been merit-based, just more "D.E.I. nonsense."

That manifested in four more firings or demotions of high-ranking women, most recently Vice Admiral Yvette Davids, the first female head of the U.S. Naval Academy.

Hegseth also dismantled the "Women, Peace, and Security" program which supported women on security teams. And famously celebrated the Iran strikes by congratulating "our boys on those bombers," seemingly oblivious to the possibility that one of the pilots was, in fact, a woman.

I wonder if Senator Ernst feels like she was played.

Women, in and out of the military, surely have taken notice of the disrespect afforded them by this administration, and the diminution of chances of promotion to higher positions. There are currently no female four-star officers on active duty, and none in line for three or four stars.

Is this going to discourage women from enrolling in the military? Would that be a step back for the military, as many believe? Obviously, Trump and Hegseth seem to think the opposite: Fewer women equates to a better military, especially in leadership roles, a complete and abrupt reversal of the previous decade's progress.

Trump famously has made derogatory statements about male war heroes and other soldiers.

As it turns out, he does not respect women in the military either.

————————

July 28, 2025
Trump's War on the Homeless: Sympathy Versus Scorn
Dear Editors,

President Donald Trump recently signed an executive order addressing homelessness that many in the field find harmful to the very people it purportedly seeks to help. The Order will move unhoused individuals into long-term institutional settings, against their will, and "enforces prohibitions on urban camping and loitering." Trump ends traditional "housing first policies."

There is no reason to think this executive order will help the unhoused. Specifically, Trump gave no details as to what type of "institutional settings" the homeless will be sent to, or how, or by whom they will be treated or helped. Given that there is already a severe shortage of psychiatric beds and psychiatrists in the United States, this new order is dishonest.

The absence of a realistic plan suggests little interest in the actual outcome, other than eliminating the eyesore and the "disorder and fear" that the homeless encampments may cause the surrounding community. Feeling safe and secure in our cities is important—but this new order serves only those of us with homes, and not those of us without.

The executive order's lack of empathy is striking. Trump describes these folks only as mentally ill, and/or as drug addicts, and/or as sex criminals that need to be evaluated for "civil commitment." There is no mention of the impoverished who cannot afford rental fees, or those who suffered domestic abuse, or other causes of homelessness unrelated to mental illness or crime. Trump seems to hold the unhoused in low esteem and blames them for their plight.

It is easy and ill-advised for those born with every advantage in life to feel superior to those who are born disadvantaged and then struggle. In particular, mental illness does not defer to wealth or success. Anyone can manifest schizophrenia or bipolar disorder, so those of us who are healthy and doing well should be grateful for that and not reflexively disparage the unhoused for their plight.

Regardless of how people end up unhoused and even if some of them made bad decisions or committed crimes, they have a difficult life: no roof, no protection from extreme heat or cold, hunger, no health care, risk of being subject to crimes, and all manner of abuse. They are human beings in dire straits and deserve our sympathy, not unmitigated scorn.

"Housing first"—which Trump rejects—has been the historical strategy for helping the unhoused by giving them a foundation to address their mental health, substance use, poverty, and other complex problems. In contrast, "Incarceration and commitment" casts them as people who need removal and does not even require their consent.

That is not just Pollyanna idealistic thinking. Project Home is a non-profit organization founded in 1989 and dedicated to reducing homelessness in Philadelphia in a humane, responsible, and non-judgmental manner. It provides "housing first," health care, addiction therapy, job opportunities, and education. Its mission statement includes "alleviating the underlying causes of poverty [...] struggles for self-esteem, recovery and confidence [...] a range of comprehensive services [...]." Project Home states that "None of us are home, until all of us are home." Its goal is to actually help the unhoused, not just get rid of them.

Trump might be surprised to learn of Project Home's success. For many reasons, helping the unhoused seems like a Sisyphean task, but for most years since its inception, Project Home has helped reduce Philadelphia's unhoused population, despite Philadelphia's high poverty rate—for example, by 27 percent from 2018 to 2022—and has been recognized as a model for reducing homelessness by multiple news organizations and a previous U.S. secretary of Housing and Urban Development.

Project Home vs. Donald Trump:
Housing over incarceration.
Healthcare over cutting Medicaid.
Sympathy over scorn.

August 9, 2025
Trump's War on Elite Law Firms Has Metastasized
Dear Editors,

President Trump's war on elite law firms is based on his ire that they have employed lawyers and represented clients and causes, including "harmful activity through their powerful *pro bono* practices," antithetical to his personal interests. He applied the power of the presidency and federal government to coerce these firms into stopping these activities. Among other things, he threatened to limit the ability of their attorneys to enter government buildings, canceled government contracts, and forbade new federal contracts.

These edicts may be illegal. Four law firms have successfully challenged these Trump orders in court.

However, nine other firms capitulated. As an attorney at one of these firms explained, the executive orders "posed an existential threat [...] could easily have destroyed (us)." In the face of those threats, the nine firms agreed to collectively provide nearly $1 billion in pro bono services to matters agreeable to Trump. Some of the agreements forbade any involvement in "DEI policies" and specified "supporting the administration's initiatives."

The greatest threat to these firms is well understood: Any behavior that Trump does not like could result, at any time and per his discretion, in further executive actions, including additional existential threats. That is, the agreements did not end the matter; they were just capitulations that satisfied Trump for the moment.

All of this means that the president of the United States named himself the functional Managing Partner at each of these private law firms, dictating their caseloads and their clients.

This cancer of the legal profession has metastasized beyond those firms. Reuters recently reported that not only have those nine firms tailored their pro bono work to specific clients and causes favorable to Trump, but this has spread throughout the legal industry. A large number of law firms have significantly cut down on pro bono services out of fear of becoming Trump's next target. They are taking no chances. Many clients are now unable to find legal representation.

The American Bar Association considers pro bono work so important that its Rules of Professional Conduct manual includes the phrase "every lawyer has a professional responsibility to provide legal services to those unable to pay." New York State even requires fifty hours of pro bono *service* as a requisite for a law license. Any diminution of pro bono services is contrary to the mission and spirit of the law. And, by definition, this focuses mostly on the poor, as they can no longer pursue legal redress for ills they perceive to have suffered.

The Trump war on elite law firms has thus evolved into a war on the poor.

———————

August 9, 2025
Trump and Performative Retribution
Dear Editors,

The Department of Justice is investigating whether New York attorney general Letitia James violated President Trump's civil rights. A recent subpoena focused on the lawsuit James filed against Trump over alleged fraud in his personal business dealings and a lawsuit she filed against the National Rifle Association.

James won both of these cases!

If Trump was serious about finding James guilty of malfeasance, he would find a case she lost. That could, at least in theory, lead to a charge of a frivolous, biased filing.

Even a kidney doctor like me can tell that an investigation into cases a district attorney won makes no sense and is going nowhere.

This recalls Trump's attempt to overthrow the results of the 2020 election. It is little remembered, but he and his attorneys filed about two dozen lawsuits that they quickly withdrew, even before any hearings. They were obviously filed just to make enough aggregate noise so that people might think "where there's smoke, there's fire." But their withdrawals clearly identified them as only smoke and no fire, a compromise Trump made by generating plenty of smoke, but getting out early enough for the lawyers to avoid misconduct findings.

The investigation of James for cases that she won is more of the same.

We are witnessing performative retribution.

———————

August 10, 2025
Trump, USAID, Contraceptives, and Sheer Hypocrisy
Dear Editors,

President Trump's administration announced plans to destroy $9.7 million of birth control pills and other contraceptives that had been funded for, manufactured, and intended for distribution by USAID to clinics in the poorest countries in Africa. This is predicted to deprive about 1.4 million women and girls of access to reproductive care. One expert predicted this will cause over 700 deaths from unsafe abortions in unwanted pregnancies, and from maternal complications in areas with minimal to no health care.

You need an extremely compelling reason to allow the deaths of so many women.

The administration's stated reason is that the contraceptives induce abortions, which the U.S. government cannot participate in. But oral contraceptives prevent pregnancies; they do not terminate them; they are not abortifacients, so the stated reason is just dishonest.

There is another layer to this, perhaps as bad. Let us presume this actually was about abortion.

Banning or disposing of actual abortifacients (if there are any involved here) would be consistent with the policy of those who are against abortion under any circumstances.

However, that is not Donald Trump's view, it is not the law in the United States, does not reflect rulings of the Supreme Court, and is not the stance of the majority of Americans.

Trump has varied his stance on abortion, but eventually settled on a middle ground on which individual states get to decide the matter for themselves. This was also the Supreme Court's ruling in overturning *Roe v. Wade*, permitting individual states to either ban or allow abortions through state legislation. After that ruling, a Trump press release bragged, "**PRESIDENT TRUMP PROMISED AND DELIVERED**: President Trump promised to protect and defend a vote of the people, from within the states, on the issue of life."

Accordingly, 38 states, a clear majority, currently allow abortions under some circumstances. Trump has supported that by refusing to support a federal ban on abortions and by publicly advocating for abortion up to 15 weeks.

Trump is saying that Americans, state by state, may decide abortion law for themselves, but Africans cannot. How does he justify allowing abortions for American women but denying them to African women? Why does Donald Trump make decisions for African women?

Why is Donald Trump so apparently unmoved by African women dying unnecessarily?

Trump's position is both hypocritical and lethal.[2]

———————

2 One obvious error with the U.S. disposal of oral contraceptives intended for Africa is that they do not induce abortions. Life is considered to begin at conception, when a sperm fertilizes an egg, and an abortion can only take place after that, not before. Oral contraceptives act by preventing ovulation, which occurs prior to conception.

However, that leads to a perhaps odd question: Are we sure that life should be defined as beginning with fertilization?

One could argue that life begins before fertilization, with oogenesis and spermatogenesis. By any definition, sperm cells and ova are living cells, with the potential under the right circumstances to end up as a human being. In that view, fertilization is simply two living cells combining to make one, an important step in the process of human life, but not an event that dwarfs everything else.

Perhaps we should also think of abortion in broader terms than commonly done now, without excess emphasis on fertilization as a defining moment. What factors should influence whether and when we can interrupt the multi-step process of generating a living organism in deference to other valid interests?

That is open for debate, but, for example, Aristotle wrote long ago, "The line between lawful and unlawful abortion will be marked by the fact of (the fetus) having sensation." The fetus develops primitive reflexes at 12 weeks and responds to external stimuli, meaning it can feel pain, by around 24 weeks. The 15-week guideline, as commonly followed in the United States, is consistent with Aristotle's teaching. I see much common sense and wisdom in that.

August 11, 2025
Trump's War on American History: The Ostrich Approach
Dear Editors,

President Trump is on a mission to rewrite American history in ways favorable to himself. The most obvious example is his recasting the Jan. 6 insurrection as an appropriate and peaceful protest against a rigged election. Thus, he pardoned the criminals and is targeting the law enforcement officials who did their jobs investigating and convicting those who stormed the Capitol.

Here are a few other examples:

Trump also, at least transiently, removed reference to his two impeachments and to Jan. 6 from an exhibit at the Smithsonian.

He issued an executive order that banned the Smithsonian from displaying exhibits that depict America's history of mistreatment of Native Americans, racism, sexism, and the like.

He objected to exhibits that referred to the Depression, the Vietnam War, and one with reference to Mickey Mouse's original blackface appearance. Can you imagine a president of the United States alarmed over Mickey Mouse's appearance?

He ordered the Interior Department to remove any descriptions from national monuments or parks that "disparaged Americans past or present."

He removed references to transgender people from the Park Service's website for the Stonewall National Monument in Greenwich Village. This is particularly odd since the riots at the Stonewall bar in 1969 essentially birthed the gay rights movement, which includes people who identify as transgender.

This recalls the apocryphal metaphor of an "ostrich sticking his head in the sand." Trump can remove almost any reference he wants by putting his head in the proverbial sand, but the things he "erases" still exist. Racism, sexism, gay- and trans-bigotry, insurrection, impeachments, and all the rest are part of history, and everyone knows that. You cannot undo history by executive order.

Furthermore, the next Democrat president is going to reverse all this senseless, futile whitewashing of American history. And I doubt that any subsequent Republican president will recapitulate Trump's childish behavior to make an endless comical cycle. So, this is all just for the moment, for Trump's personal gratification, and for his audience.

The president of the United States should not behave like an ostrich.

August 15, 2025
DOGE, Deportations, and D.C.: The Same Thing Over and Over Again.
Dear Editors,

Three of President Trump's important initiatives—DOGE, deportations, and taking control of the District of Columbia—follow the same narrative arc and demonstrate his standard operating procedure.

It goes something like this:

First, Trump invents a national emergency that requires him to intervene as an unsolicited White Knight. He does so without formal study, without considering relevant data, and without any nuance or attempt at wisdom. He goes full battle mode, acts first, thinks later.

Then, he delivers just a fraction of what he promised. In the process, he injures a lot of people.

When the project ends, sometimes before it ends, with the harm greater than the benefit, he announces its great success.

Start with DOGE. Trump and Elon Musk declared that we had $2 trillion waste in the federal budget that they could and would eliminate. Musk then fired people and ended programs seemingly randomly, rather than with an informed, data-based, targeting of actual waste.

When he was done, Musk claimed to have saved around $50 billion, just 2.5 percent of the original projection. Worse yet, others who studied the matter concluded that when you included costs, legal reversals, eventual re-hirings, and Musk's accounting legerdemain, the actual savings were just a couple billion dollars, about 1/1000 of the original claim, and as little as 0.03 percent of the approximately $7 trillion federal budget. Financially, a non-event!

As for the injuries caused, it is estimated that 200,000 federal workers lost their jobs, and their families continue to feel the pain.

Trump called this a huge success.

What about Trump's mass deportations? Here, Trump declared a national emergency by claiming that America was being overrun by hordes of immigrant gangsters, rapists, and murderers. On multiple occasions, he stressed that his mass deportation policy would focus on violent criminals, "the worst of the worst."

No president ever had a policy to allow violent immigrant criminals to stay; they have always been deported. So the relevant metric for Trump's success is how many additional violent criminals did his administration deport? As of late June, the number of deportees convicted of a violent crime had only increased from 5,300 last year to 7,700 this year. Every deported violent criminal is a good thing, but this, too, was just a fraction of what Trump promised. It meant that his premise that America was overrun by these people was pure fiction.

As for the damage done? Trump never bothered to even try to target violent criminals; instead, he established daily quotas. It turned out that only 7 percent of deportees had committed violent crimes and the rest had committed only minor, nonviolent crimes, or even no crime at all. In fact, the number of deportees without any criminal record increased by about 50,000 compared with last year! The damage done to those people, their families, and their communities was vast. How many children of immigrants were once again, as in Trump's first administration, separated from their parents? Far too many, for sure, with one change from then to now: In Trump's first term, some of the children were put in cages, whereas in Trump's second term, some of the parents were put in cages.

Once again, Trump called this a huge success.

Finally, to the District of Columbia, where Trump declared a "violent crime crisis," despite data indicating otherwise. He sent troops in as a reflexive response to a carjacking. Already, the results are far short of promised. FBI director Kash Patel announced today that since 1,600 federal personnel were sent to D.C. several days ago, only 120 people, out of a population of 700,000, have been arrested. Only two were homicide suspects. Many of those 120 might have been arrested without the federal intervention, and we do not know how many actually committed crimes, or how many will eventually be released without charges.

Many of those arrested were simply illegal immigrants who had committed no crime besides their entry. They, too, were not part of a "violent crime crisis"; they were actually bothering no one.

Worse yet, we can be sure that damage is being done in this process, to people wrongly arrested, to their families, to the community.

Trump is already calling this a huge success.

DOGE, deportations, and D.C.: The same sad story over and over again.

——————————

August 31, 2025
Trump's War on Unions: It Boggles the Mind
Dear Editors,

When someone provides an obviously false explanation for something they have done, you usually can smell a rat. This describes President Trump's war on unions.

This war began with Trump's executive order on March 27, 2025, that broke up unions at over 30 government agencies, based on Trump's declaration that they were national security risks. This was the largest single action of union-busting in American history.

When and how did unions become national security risks? At a minimum, such a claim should involve unions related to the armed forces or government agencies involved in national security, but as it turned out, that was not the case here. For many of these agencies, Trump's claims of national security risk seem fabricated to advance his agenda.

One of Trump's major targets was the Veterans Administration, which, following his orders, terminated union contracts involving almost 400,000 employees. The VA provides a variety of benefits, including disability services and health care, to veterans and their families. Can you imagine VA unions, which advocate for those who served our country, as a risk to national security? In what way?

If there was any question about how dubious Trump's national security claims are, and there should not have been any, it was answered when Trump signed another executive order ending collective bargaining agreements with more government agencies, including the United States Agency for Global Media, the Office of the Commissioner for Patents, and areas of the Bureau of Reclamation that operate hydroelectric power plants. Hard to call unions of those agencies national security risks with a straight face.

It turns out that Trump had previously provided the real explanation for his war on unions, but it was buried in a White House Fact Sheet issued back in March and went mostly unnoticed. From the desk of the president:

> Certain Federal unions have declared war on President Trump's agenda. The largest Federal union describes itself as "fighting back" against Trump. It is widely filing grievances to block Trump policies. For example, VA's unions have filed 70 national and local grievances over President Trump's policies since the inauguration—an average of over one a day.

So, Trump's actual beef, per his own telling, is that unions have some power, and that they sometimes use that power to "fight back" against perceived injustices, often against something Trump has done, or something that helps Trump achieve a specific goal. In Trump's world, that is not permitted. So the unions must be broken up, and if you need an absurd pretense like national security to do so [...] well, whatever works. Verdict first, rationale to follow.

Most of this is easily understood through Trump's quest for unlimited power and his view of power in the world as a zero-sum game. In his view, the less power the other guy has, the more power he has.

But even that fails to explain some of these anti-union dictums. For example, for what possible reason would Trump target the patent office? Certainly not for national security reasons, and the patent office has no political power and poses no threat to him.

Some of this just boggles the mind.

———————

September 1, 2025
Trump Undermines His War on Opium
Dear Editors,

Donald Trump deserves some credit: In 2017, he was the first president to declare opium-related deaths a national emergency. He did not instigate any particularly effective action at that time—the incidence of overdose deaths increased during his first term—but at least he shined a light on the problem.

Fortunately, during President Biden's term, the incidence of overdose deaths leveled off in 2022 and 2023, and finally decreased in 2024, down almost 27 percent from the previous year. According to the CDC, this was due to expanded access to Narcan, an opioid antagonist, as well as to enhanced substance abuse treatments.

With Trump's return to power, and his frequent rhetorical focus on the opioid problem, perhaps we should hope for continued improvement.

Not so quick.

Nearly two-thirds of patients getting outpatient treatment for opioid addiction are on Medicaid, so Trump's $1 trillion cut of Medicaid funding unfortunately jeopardizes their coverage for treatment. Recognizing this as a major problem, Congress included a provision in the Big, Beautiful, Bill to exclude people with substance use disorders from the Medicaid work requirement. But they still need to navigate ever stricter bureaucratic processes in order to maintain their insurance. Many will surely fall between the cracks as Medicaid is slashed.

Furthermore, rural hospitals and clinics reliant on Medicaid reimbursement are at risk of eliminating services or even closing, further reducing available addiction treatment options.

How many people will lose their substance abuse treatments? How many will lose access to Narcan? How many will die as a result? Too many!

President Trump had competing interests in devising the latest government budget: For instance, tax breaks, mostly for the wealthy, vs. funds for Medicaid, including for substance abuse treatments. His priorities became clear. He chose the tax breaks.

The war on opioids requires more funding, not less. This is a worthy cause that should not be diminished in any way. Yet Trump diminished it.

Trump is undermining his own war on opiods.

——————————

October 4, 2025
Trump's Fake War on Drugs
Dear Editors,

In response to accusations from legal scholars that the killings of alleged Venezuelan drug dealers in international waters were extrajudicial, presidentially sanctioned murders, President Trump declared that the people he had ordered killed were armed, threatening combatants, and that the killings were allowed by the laws of war. Actually, these people appear to have been unarmed and far out in international waters, not even close to Trump's characterization. It seems that Trump simply imagines his own reality to suit his own purposes. (Similarly, Trump described Portland as a "burning hellhole" even though Portland ranks 72nd in the country in the incidence of violent crime.)

Furthermore, there are many thousands of drug traffickers (12,000 convictions in the United States in 2024 alone) and only 20 percent of those convicted were foreign, so these international killings are just a drop in the bucket of total suppliers. As long as there is a huge demand and the business is lucrative, there will be plenty of people, both in America and around the world, who will meet that demand and will take risks in doing so. Trump cannot kill or even deter more than a tiny fraction of them. His plan to win the war on drugs solely by killing suppliers is doomed from the start.

Thus, killing a handful of international drug traffickers every week or two is not only extrajudicial, it is pointless—merely for show and Trump's personal aggrandizement—and that makes the extrajudicial aspect even worse.

A sensible war on drugs must address demand. Unfortunately, funding Medicaid, mental health programs, drug rehabilitation, early education, child care, and similar social programs takes years to yield any benefits, and that does not suit Trump's needs; it does not make him look and feel powerful, as the killings do. Instead, he disparages these common-sense approaches with his usual reflexive pejoratives, including, for example, calling them radical, socialist, and DEI—promoting. He actually slashed relevant funding, the opposite of what he would do if he really cared about the drug problem.

As long as Trump persists in wasteful and murderous efforts to diminish the supply of drugs, with zero interest in addressing the demand, he is waging a fake war on drugs.

———————

December 12, 2025
Yes, the President Can Get Away With Murder
(Published in the *Chicago Tribune*)
Dear Editors,

When the U.S. Supreme Court majority ruled in *Trump v. United States* that a president has "absolute immunity from criminal prosecution for actions within his conclusive and preclusive constitutional authority," Justice Sonia Sotomayor dissented, noting, among other things, that the ruling would allow the president to commit murder. As an example, she wrote that if the president "orders the Navy's Seal Team 6 to assassinate a political rival? Immune."

To many, her comment seemed extreme—reductio ad absurdum. No president of the United States would ever order a murder.

But now we have President Donald Trump ordering the killing of unarmed boat occupants far from our border. Law professor Gabor Rona, echoing many other legal scholars, recently wrote that "these killings are simply murder–extrajudicial killings in violation of United States and international human rights law because the boats' occupants are not attacking the United States, nor do they pose an immediate threat of attack."

That seems pretty straightforward. It seems like the decision to kill was made first, and then a justification—any justification, even if preposterous—was then sought.

Sotomayor's thinking now seems prescient. Indeed, the president of the United States can get away with murder.

CHAPTER 13

TRUMP'S TARIFFS AND THE ECONOMY

May 7, 2025
Trump's Economic Plan: Buy Less Toys
Dear Editors,

Donald Trump's economic plan emphasizes high tariffs and large tax cuts and comes with his promise that prices will come down fast, inflation will end, unemployment will decrease, businesses will flock to America, and our economy will become "the greatest ever." Basically, he guarantees great gain and no pain. However, many economic experts across the country do not buy that.

Despite that criticism, many Republican politicians still expressed support for tariffs, albeit often guarded, along the lines of "Trump is the President, it's his call, let's wait and see."

The initial "wait and see" period is over. As most economic experts predicted, prices are rising, GDP declined, the dollar is weaker, the stock market plummeted, and retirement accounts shrank. Perhaps that will change for the better, but importantly, this week, even Trump acknowledged the recent economic decline. Then he advised Americans to ease their pain by "buying less toys," which seemed a tone-deaf response and remarkably devoid of empathy coming from a billionaire.

It is still early and the stock market is notoriously resilient, but "buy less toys" suggests that even Trump is concerned about the initial results of his economic plan.

———————————

July 10, 2025
Trump's Tariffs are Not About the Economy
Dear Editors,

President Trump's tariffs have been broadly criticized by economists as being bad economic policy. However, today we saw evidence that the tariffs are not about the economy, at least not all of them.

Trump just pledged a 50 percent tariff on Brazil for prosecuting his insurrectionist friend Jair Bolsonaro's attempt to overturn his 2022 election loss. That led to Brazilian president da Silva's precious response, "[…] if Trump was Brazilian and did what he did at the Capitol, he'd be on trial in Brazil for violating the Constitution." Neither the threat nor the reply had anything to do with economics. We have had a trade surplus with Brazil for the past 18 years.

Similarly, we have had a trade surplus with the United Kingdom for 19 years, yet Trump has threatened to increase their tariff nearly ten-fold.

Trump also pledged tariffs on a variety of countries, most of them on the poor side—Libya, Iraq, Algeria, Sri Lanka, Moldova, Brunei, and the Philippines—whose collective trade imbalance with the United States is around 18 billion dollars—a rounding error, given our gross national product of $30 trillion. Obviously, that will have no real effect on our economy. What is really going on here?[1]

These tariffs are simply an expression of Trump's presidential power, what he can do, without an actual economic or governing philosophy backing them up. And if they lead to increased prices in America, as most experts project, it is just collateral economic damage to the rest of us.

————————

1 Nearly one month later, President Trump raised tariffs on India as punishment for India "buying massive amounts of Russian oil […].They don't care how many people in Ukraine are being killed by the Russian War Machine." This provided another example where he uses tariffs as a political tool to try to get what he wants, to punish countries, wholly unrelated to any American economic issues.

July 31, 2025
Do Tariffs Have Hidden Costs? Time Will Tell.
Dear Editors,

Earlier this week President Trump announced a trade deal with the European Union that was widely seen as favorable to the United States. This supported and reinforced his "capitulate or tariff" style.

The next couple of days were not as good. First, Fed chairman Jerome Powell refused to lower interest rates out of concern for creeping inflation. Then, deals could not be reached with dozens of other countries including Canada and Mexico, so Trump announced a blitz of tariffs, overall more than seven times higher than one year ago.

One day later, the July job market data was released indicating that the number of jobs added was the lowest in more than four years. There was also a downward revision of over a quarter million jobs previously reported for May and June. Quickly, the stock market dropped.

So, it is fair to say the results of Trump's economic plan are unsettled for now; many economic experts remain concerned.

Time will tell.

That is the quantitative part. But I wonder if there is more to this. Are there hidden costs to "capitulate or tariff?" Trump is the most powerful man in the world, and he is exerting that power—do what I say or suffer the consequences—on a daily basis. How will other countries react to this in the future? Is there a reason no other president in the history of the United States has ever acted in this fashion? Will foreign countries respond by slowly moving their trade elsewhere, by strengthening other relationships?

Nobody likes being bullied. Could the loss of camaraderie, the loss of respect, the loss of trust, and the outright abuse backfire on the United States? As sovereign countries reconsider their international options and international partners, will their support for the United States wane?

It is quite possible that the short-term economic effects of Trump's "capitulate or tariff" approach may have long-term unintended consequences that will diminish our position or influence and respect in the world. If so, definitely not a good trade-off.

Time will tell.

———————

August 2, 2025
Are Trump's Tariffs Legal?
Dear Editors,

There is an interesting ongoing legal battle about Trump's tariffs that has been lost in all the recent tumult about trade deals, unprecedented tariffs slapped on other countries, a bad jobs report, and the firing of the Bureau of Labor Statistics commissioner.

That battle involves five American businesses and 12 states that have sued Trump on the basis that his tariffs are illegal. They argue that the power to invoke tariffs, the so-called power of the purse, lies with Congress, and that Trump has overstepped his constitutional authority.

A federal appeals court is currently reviewing a lower court ruling that sided with the plaintiffs.

Trump's Justice Department attorney claimed in the appeals court that his tariffs address a "national emergency" and that "Congress has long given the president broad discretion" in that area. In this instance, Trump claims that our trade deficit and the flow of fentanyl into the country from Canada add up to a national emergency.

In response, plaintiff's lawyer argued that Trump had asserted a "breathtaking claim to power that no president has asserted in 200 years."

The initial questioning and commentary of the appeals court judges suggested they may side with the plaintiffs. One judge admonished a Trump lawyer, "You are asking for an unbounded authority," reiterating the plaintiff's position.

For sure, the president must have the authority to declare national emergencies in wartime and for similar dire circumstances. Does a trade deficit constitute a national emergency? Many economists do not even see trade deficits as a problem.

The potential problem with giving a president the unregulated power to declare a national emergency—no review, no checks and balances—is that a dishonest, unstable, or immoral president can use that to justify anything that happens to suit his political or personal needs.

Will the Supreme Court justices find a way, when this case reaches them, to enforce the historical checks and balances that define a democracy? Or will they give Trump carte blanche to declare national emergencies to allow him to do almost anything?

Seems like their decision will transcend the tariff issue.

————————

August 4, 2025
The Tariffs Are a Con Job
Dear Editors,

President Trump recently bragged that his tariffs are bringing in billions to the U.S. economy. So much money that he and his colleagues are talking about how to best utilize it. Senator Josh Hawley (R-MO) suggested a cash rebate and even introduced legislation authorizing $600 per person. Alternatively, Trump suggested using the money to pay down the skyrocketing national debt.

Both options involve some considerable chicanery.

Economists, and economic history, predict that tariffs will be paid for mostly by American consumers. Inflation is already creeping up, and explains why Jerome Powell, chair of the Federal Reserve, refuses to bow to Trump's demand to cut interest rates. Many companies have done their best to keep prices down, but profit margins being so thin, companies can only do so much for so long; many have announced plans to raise prices. Furthermore, many more tariffs, some quite steep, have just been levied. With that combination of factors, economists expect consumers to bear more and more of the cost of tariffs as time goes by.

Therefore, if Trump gives rebates derived from tariff revenue, he will be returning to consumers the money that he took from consumers. Tariff revenue comes disproportionately from people with less means, since they spend a higher proportion of their income on goods and services. Therefore, Trump will be taking from the poor in order to give back to the poor. That may seem to those involved merely a hardship partially resolved, but Trump will celebrate it as a benevolent act that justifies the tariffs. That will be disingenuous, if not frankly deceitful.

It gets worse, since Hawley's rebate idea has not caught on. Trump seems more likely to use tariff revenue to pay down the national debt, and that is even sketchier.

Trump's tax cuts go predominantly to the wealthy, and that increases the national debt. Using tariff revenue mostly from the less well-off to pay down the debt allows for maximal tax relief for the wealthy. It is the equivalent of taking from the poor and giving to the rich.

Take from the poor and give to the poor, or, take from the poor and give to the rich. Either way, I wonder whether people will get wise to Trump's con job.

CHAPTER 14

THE ENVIRONMENT

July 7, 2025
Make China Great Again
Dear Editors,

Lost in the uproar about other aspects of Trump's "Big, Beautiful Bill" is its head-in-the-sand approach to renewable energy. Elon Musk may be way off-kilter many times (see DOGE), but he is also a proven innovator so perhaps he is on to something when he says that Trump's bill is "utterly insane and destructive. It gives handouts to industries of the past while severely damaging industries of the future." Musk is referring to Trump's bromance with petroleum, natural gas, and coal, his promise to his base to return to the mid-twentieth century (the "Again" in MAGA) when those industries ruled the earth, while at the same time mocking the energy of the future—hydropower, solar, and wind.

This reflects, of course, Trump's antipathy to climate change issues and clean energy, but it is also a potential calamity in the area most near and dear to him—the economy. Trump is glorifying the less efficient ways of the past, while disparaging a more modern approach. The firm Energy Innovation predicted that wholesale energy prices in America will increase 50 percent by 2035. By 2030, annual consumer energy costs will increase $16 billion, and almost a million energy-related jobs will be lost.

China is taking the opposite approach, leaping into the future via renewable energy sources. Thus, the economic prosperities of China and the United States may diverge, which will have many ramifications, none of them good for us.

As *New York Times* op-ed writer Thomas Friedman observed, Trump is "Making China Great Again."

July 15, 2025
Is FEMA Horrible? Or Really Great?
Dear Editors,

President Trump visited Texas after heavy rainfall caused the Guadalupe River in Kerr County to rise 26 feet in less than an hour, killing at least 121.

This served as an ironic reminder that Trump plans to eliminate FEMA, after already cutting funds and firing employees at the EPA, the National Weather Service, the U.S. Geological Survey, the Interior Department, the National Oceanic and Atmospheric Administration, and others. All of that without any prior study or careful decision-making, just slash-and-gash seemingly based on random target goals for employees fired and salaries saved.

Oddly, there was a time when Trump was a huge FEMA fan. In storm-ravaged Puerto Rico in 2017, he said, "We have done a great job [...]. People are now starting to recognize the amazing work that has been done by FEMA [...]." Add that to similar comments about the FEMA responses to hurricanes that year in Texas and Florida.

People in the field, not surprisingly, believe that Trump's current agenda will ravage our ability to predict and warn of disasters, mitigate them in advance, and respond both immediately and down the line to help those suffering. That may have already started. There are reports that FEMA could not answer all the calls from Texas because it had fired hundreds of call center contractors. FEMA has already lost about a quarter of its full-time staff. Some say the FEMA response in Texas was late.

Furthermore, Kristi Noem, Trump's secretary of Homeland Security, cut the FEMA budget by requiring that every grant and contract over the relatively small amount of $100,000 require her personal approval. As a result, $3.6 billion in grants from FEMA to hundreds of communities has already been revoked.

We had a series of devastating floods this year, with Kentucky, West Virginia, and Tennessee preceding Texas. Is this an area in which a sensible person slashes relevant funding and fires workers?

At any rate, the idea that FEMA is inept, wasteful, and should be cut back or disbanded was just disputed in Texas, by, of all people, Republicans. Governor Greg Abbott lauded the federal response to the flooding, "There has been extraordinary collaboration with the state and the federal government to make sure that we address Texans' needs as quickly as possible through disaster assistance programs. The State of Texas will continue to work with our federal and local partners." Trump concurred, "When the request was made for the emergency funds [...] we gave it within about two minutes, maybe less, and they had everything they needed right [*sic*] immediately."

That is, both Trump and Abbott lauded the performance of the agency that Trump plans to shut down due to incompetence. Who would have predicted that?

Perhaps Trump will reconsider ending FEMA. Or at least holding off on his scorched earth approach. If not, I feel for anyone who lives in an earthquake, flood, hurricane, or tornado-prone area [...] pretty much most of us.

———————

July 25, 2025
Trump's War on the Environment
Dear Editors,

The United Nations' (UN) highest judicial body, the International Court of Justice, just unanimously (15 judges) announced that member nations must protect people from the "urgent and existential threat" of climate change, and that failure to do so would constitute "an intentionally wrongful act." This is a legal ruling stating that actions harmful to the environment violate international law. The Court also ruled that government support of fossil-fuel production is a potential "violation of the principle of ensuring human rights."

At the same time, the European Union and China—two rather disparate ideologies—issued a joint statement at a summit meeting re-endorsing the Paris

Agreement as "the cornerstone of international climate cooperation," and asking that "[...] all countries [...] step up efforts to address climate change."

These statements reflect the reality that probably 95 percent of climate scientists in 99 percent of the countries in the world recognize climate change as a huge threat.

One significant exception to the international consensus and fervor is President Donald Trump's America. Trump calls climate change "a hoax" and has long waged a multipronged war on the environment. This included withdrawing from the Paris Agreement, and more recently, terminating billions of dollars for EPA grants, shutting down its Office of Research and Development, firing numerous employees (with a stated goal of reducing the EPA workforce by 65 percent), and now announcing that they seek to overturn an important 2009 EPA "endangerment finding" that served as the foundation for many rules and policies that addressed climate change.

Most of the entire world is calling for increased efforts to combat climate change, and the United States alone is doing just the opposite.

This is not well-explained by Trump's usual "The experts are not experts. I am the expert." Trump has never publicly discussed environmental data, studies, or any actual evidence behind his disagreements with the world's scientists. I doubt anyone believes he has actually read any scientific papers or even listened closely to any scientific presentations on the subject. His claim of hoax does not seem based on much of anything.

Instead, it seems like Trump found a cause célèbre that appeals to his base and perhaps makes him feel and look both brilliant and powerful. It also fits into the overall Trump motif of denying expert opinion, science, and evidence whenever he can, and endorsing the opposite position in order to fuel his perceived self-interest. In that construct, neither the evidence nor the science even matter. His base predictably responds to that message and he revels in his peculiar brand of contrarian thinking.

Repealing all sorts of environmental regulations and restrictions should provide financial benefits to coal, oil, and related industries, just as Trump promised. But the rest of the world, including China, realizes that these industries are in decline and the future is elsewhere, so those benefits will be just short term. Not a compelling reason to risk continued climate change damage.

As the Trump war on the environment proceeds, we better hope that Trump is right, and the world's scientists are wrong. Because, if not, we are all in a heap of trouble.

———————

August 3, 2025
Denying Climate Change: Five Men Against the World
Dear Editors,

President Trump's newly slimmed down EPA—he dismissed hundreds of scientists who disagreed with his opinion that climate change is a hoax—announced that the EPA's 2009 declaration, called the "endangerment finding," is scientifically and legally invalid and going to be rescinded.

The "endangerment finding" was a bedrock scientific statement, based on overwhelming evidence and supported by scientists around the world. Its take-home message is that planet-warming greenhouse gases pose a threat to public health. This allowed previous administrations to place limits on greenhouse gas emissions from cars, power plants, and other sources of pollution. Renouncing this declaration will gut efforts to address climate change—that is the point of doing so.

The EPA cited the contrary opinion of five scientists, already known for their anti-climate change thinking, expressed in a report issued by the Energy Department.

I am not a climate scientist, but it looks to me that this alleged scientific disagreement could be summarized as follows: five handpicked people versus the rest of the scientific world.

CHAPTER 15

TRUMP AND EPSTEIN

July 28, 2025
Trump Is a Cause of Epstein-mania
Dear Editors,

Epstein-mania rolls on and President Trump continues to complain that it is all a "democratic con job […] another hoax," nothing to see here, move on.

Commentator Fareed Zaharia makes the point that "Donald Trump is the main character in this story, having come to power and returned to power after aggressively promoting birtherism, election fraud and many other conspiracies. He has also brought into the mainstream people like Alex Jones and Kash Patel, who have trafficked in even more extreme theories and insinuations […]. Michael Flynn, Trump's first national security adviser, spread the lie that Hillary Clinton was connected to child sex rings […]."

No president in American history has trafficked in conspiracy theories and bizarre allegations like Donald Trump. Not surprisingly, he has stirred much of his base to think likewise, or, those who think likewise have become much of his base. They see conspiracies everywhere, especially among high-ranking government officials and organizations. Now, Trump's people are in charge. It is going to be hard to blame the Democrats when Trump and the Republicans are running just about everything and the Democrats run just about nothing.

However, this plays out, Trump fueled it.

————————

August 3, 2025
Trump Clarifies His Beef with Epstein
Dear Editors,

President Trump recently clarified that he did not end his friendship with Jeffrey Epstein, as Trump originally stated, because Epstein was a "creep" who "liked girls on the young side." Epstein eventually was convicted of sexual trafficking those underage girls, which may have been obvious, or at least suspected, all along.

But apparently that was not Trump's problem with Epstein.

Instead, Trump explained that Epstein "[…] was taking people from (Trump's) spa […]. I told him, we don't want you taking our people […]. Then he did it again. And I said, 'out of here.'" Per Trump's own telling, he could abide Epstein's interest in young girls but not Epstein's lack of business ethics.

It is good to be honest, but that has to be one of the most self-indicting clarifications we have ever heard.

————————

August 4, 2025
Trump and a Maxwell Pardon? Don't Forget Jan. 6
Dear Editors,

Ghislaine Maxwell, Jeffrey Epstein's partner and convicted sex trafficker, is talking to President Trump's deputy attorney general Todd Blance, obviously hoping for a reduced sentence, a pardon, or some other favorable treatment.

Trump was recently asked about the pardon.

Both the question and his answer—"I'm allowed to do it, but it's something I have not thought about"—spoke ill of him.

Pardoning a sex trafficker and abuser of young women who has barely started her sentence and expressed no remorse is outrageous. Trump's answer should have been, "NO WAY." End of that story, rather than an equivocation which suggested a pardon was a possibility.

The idea is so preposterous that no other president would even have been asked about it. Trump was asked because it is understood as, for this president, plausible. After all, although there have been bad pardons before (e.g., Bill Clinton pardoned fugitive felon Mark Rich), Trump is the author of the most notorious, unforgivable pardons of all time: the Jan. 6 rioters.

More than a thousand of those folks pled guilty, and of the 261 indicted rioters who completed their trial, 98.5 percent were found guilty. That is what happens when you storm the Capitol in plain sight to prevent a congressional proceeding; there is no defense, not even in front of Trump-appointed judges.

Yet Trump called these prosecutions a "grave national injustice that has been perpetrated upon the American people." And then he pardoned the criminals.

The explanation for that absurdity is obvious. Trump directed these criminals to the Capitol for the purpose of continuing his unsavory effort to remain president even though he had lost the election. They were Trump loyalists, and Trump rewarded their loyalty. In Trump's mind, loyalty overrides a heinous crime.

Maxwell, of course, knows all of this and understands her unique opportunity. Trump has been increasingly tainted by his prior Epstein affiliation, and she could help sanitize that, at least in terms of public relations. She could tell Blance, for eventual public release, some variation of Trump had nothing to do with the sex trafficking, did not know anything about it, did not hang out with underage girls, and actually was a very well-behaved gentleman at all times.

That would obviously be self-serving for her, but it would demonstrate fealty to Trump. We know how highly Trump values loyalty, almost above everything else—and even a little bit goes a long way.

As scandalous as a Maxwell pardon would be, Trump's Jan. 6 pardons tell us that it is a possibility.

———————

September 9, 2025
The Epstein Drawing: Trump is the Architect of his Own Problems
Dear Editors,

The House Oversight Committee just released a sexually suggestive drawing of a naked woman's torso, with writing on it that befit the drawing, apparently sent by President Trump to Jeffrey Epstein as a birthday note in 2003. It was juvenile, and it suggested juvenile cavortings at Epstein's parties, but there was no crime or even terrible misdeed particularly suggested. A 56-year-old man seemingly behaved like a teenager. Not flattering, but not unusual, and not the most damning thing ever heard. Actually, nothing specifically damning of Trump, with regards to his friendship with Epstein, has ever been alleged. In particular, no one has alleged that Trump associated with any of the underage girls who Epstein trafficked.

Trump could have limited this to a transient embarrassment with a response along the lines of "yes, but it was more than two decades ago, I was a different person then, I regret some of my behavior back then, but I did not hurt anyone, I am a much more serious and mature man now, and I am committed to making America great again." If he had said that, how long would this story continue to taint him? At least this drawing's 15 minutes of fame would already have ended.

But that is not Trump. He is not capable of admitting anything that is the slightest bit unfavorable to him. Instead, he sued the *Wall Street Journal* for their initial reporting on the birthday letter. At that time, he called the drawing, like everything else averse to him, fake. The signature, which resembled other examples of Trump signatures, was fake. He did not do drawings, though other drawings surfaced. He did not do drawings of women, as if that was a personal taboo. He did everything except deal with the issue in a rational, mature way that could have removed him from the drama.

The White House's immediate response to the drawing simply iterated those points. Trump followed suit, like a one-trick pony. He threatened to sue the *New York Times* for their reporting. His modus operandi is deny, deny, deny, insult, and sue.

In both his personal life and in his role as president, Trump's dishonesty and ego are often the architect and the fuel on the fire of his own problems. He has never learned that honesty and contrition can go far. That is unfortunate, as the nature of his entire presidency would have been much for the better, had he ever incorporated those basic character traits.

CHAPTER 16

TRUMP TAKES OVER THE DISTRICT OF COLUMBIA

August 11, 2025
Trump, D.C., and Liberty Valance
Dear Editors,

President Trump announced plans for a federal takeover of Washington D.C. in order to address a "public safety emergency."

Prior to this, Trump had behaved in the opposite fashion, a thorn in fighting crime in D.C. He cut funding to D.C. by $1 billion and gutted the U.S. Attorney's office by firing many attorneys and other office personnel who worked on Special Prosecutor Jack Smith's team or on other Jan. 6 cases. They have not been replaced. His own appointee for the U.S. attorney for D.C., Jeanine Pirro, publicly complained that "I'm down 90 prosecutors, 60 investigators and paralegals."

However, after a carjacking and assault on two citizens, Trump abruptly took a U-turn and went ballistic about crime in D.C., characterizing it as "totally out of control [...] thugs randomly attacking, mugging, maiming, and shooting innocent citizens."

The problem with Trump's sudden declaration of an emergency in D.C. is that it is false. Crime in D.C. has actually decreased this year, 26 percent for violent crime—the lowest rate in thirty years!—with similar declines in robbery, assault with a deadly weapon, murder, and rape. That is one reason no one in D.C. has asked for Trump's help.

Make no mistake, the crime rate is still too high. However, a high crime rate is not sufficient reason for a federal takeover; by law, that requires an emergency. In the prior 30 years when the crime rate was even higher than it is now, including the four years of Trump's first term, neither he nor any other president ordered the National Guard into D.C., or took over the police force. How did a single carjacking convert an improving situation into an emergency?[1]

This was not a sudden emergency that led to an intervention. It was first and foremost a decision to intervene for personal reasons, and then declare an emergency because that was required to justify the intervention.

Trump ignored the decline in D.C. crime because it neither serves his false narrative nor facilitates his strongman agenda. His mantra is that America is breaking down, crime is rampant everywhere, and "only I can fix it." He maintains that story because if it ain't broke, then we do not need him to fix it.

He has not yet called the improved D.C. crime data "rigged," as he did the recent weak jobs report.[2] Instead, he just presents, over and over again, his fictitious emergency crime wave as fact.

This recalls the famous line from the movie *The Man Who Shot Liberty Valance*: "When the legend becomes fact, print the legend."

————————

1 One question about President Trump's takeover of D.C. is "Why today?" Why not last week or any time since his inauguration? Why did this one carjacking and assault prompt federal intervention? I wonder something really odd, whether the widely reported online moniker of one of the victims—"Big Balls"—contributed. Not because of Trump's well-known puerile fixation with "big hands" or "small hands" and other childish insinuations (the animated TV show "South Park" portrays Trump with a tiny penis, knowing that upsets him). However, the media, particularly television, seemed to think "Big Balls" was a hook for national viewers; seemingly every report of the assault included the moniker, even though it had zero news value. That hook may have changed the story from local news—a single carjacking—which Trump would not have noticed, to a national story which almost everyone noticed. Trump took advantage of an already attentive nation to proclaim a public safety emergency. If "Big Balls" did indeed contribute, even indirectly, to the federal takeover of D.C., that would be an example of "truth is stranger than fiction."

2 It took almost two weeks, but as predicted, Trump eventually claimed that "D.C. gave Fake Crime numbers in order to create a false illusion of safety."

August 13, 2025.
Trump's Wars on the Homeless and on D.C.: He Applies Make-Up
Dear Editors,

President Trump sent federal troops into the District of Columbia on the basis that D.C. had a public safety emergency and was "taken over by violent gangs and bloodthirsty criminals." He then used the pretense of overwhelming crime as cover to extend his war on the homeless, who were mostly staying in encampments and minding their own business. They were not close to bloodthirsty or violent, mostly just sad souls with nowhere else to go.

President Trump's coinciding wars on D.C. crime and on the D.C. homeless share some important features.

The people he is targeting largely belong to minorities.

They live in a locale that did not vote for Trump.

But most importantly, in both areas, he is getting rid of people, rather than helping them. Get them off the streets, to somewhere they cannot be seen, to unspecified institutions for the homeless, and to jail for criminals.

If Trump was interested in reducing crime and homelessness in D.C., he would at least try to address the root causes of crime and homelessness, rather than ignore them. A root-cause approach for both would include, variably, permanent supportive housing, robust mental health services, targeted economic support, emphasis on education and child care, and rehabilitation. None of which Trump is doing anywhere in the country, not for crime, and not for homelessness.

Trump's approach to both crime and homelessness addresses appearances, but not problems. He simply removes people from sight, which is like putting make-up on skin cancer. It is an illusion and not a solution.

————————

August 14, 2025
Trump's War on No-Cash Bail: Very Little Knowledge Is Very Dangerous
Dear Editors,

After invading D.C. with the National Guard and taking over the police force, President Trump suggested that Chicago is next on his list.

Trump expressed his outrage over Illinois' no-cash bail policy, enacted in 2023. He provided no data to support any negative results of the policy; he simply fear-mongered with the claim that "Every place in the country where you have no-cash bail is a disaster" and "Somebody murders somebody and they're out on no-cash bail before the day is out." He seemed unaware of the decrease in violent crime in Chicago in 2025—greater than 30 percent, with homicide at its lowest incidence since 2014. He also seemed unaware of national data from the Brennan Center for Justice that found "no statistically significant relationship between bail reform and crime rates" in 33 cities. Trump's stated link between the no-cash bail policy and crime? He just made it up. And it gets worse.

Trump does not seem to have even an elementary understanding of how accused criminals are processed, and what no-cash bail policy actually does and does not do.

After an arrest, the criminal justice system must balance the opposing principles of "innocent until proven guilty" versus the possibility that alleged criminals could be a threat to the community. The first provides impetus to release the accused on the sensible basis that innocent people (as the pre-trial accused are) should not spend time in jail. The second idea, also sensible, suggests that in order to protect the community, people who might commit serious crimes after release should not be released, an understandably major priority.

The presiding judge determines whether the accused can be safely released or not. There are several criteria judges generally follow, depending on the jurisdiction. The most important is that many crimes are considered automatically "detainable offenses." That, of course, includes murder. People accused of murder are not released, contrary to Trump's claim. Judges also consider the particular facts of a case, a defendant's past criminal or psychological history as well as other factors. If the accused has committed a detainable offense, or if the judge, after hearing the opposing legal arguments, determines that the defendant is a risk to the community, then he remains incarcerated pending trial.

A second step may follow, but only if, and after, the judge has determined that the defendant is not a risk to the community and may be released. In that event, the judge sets bail. The point of bail, whether cash or no-cash, is to motivate the accused to return for court rather than skip town. That is, bail is about flight risk; bail has nothing to do with the risk of committing crimes after release, as the judgment about that has already been made.

The cash requirement for bail is widely considered problematic. Poor people who cannot meet a cash bail requirement remain in jail even though they have been judged no risk to the community. This is why much of the rest of the world has no-cash bail policies. These policies are not, despite what Trump says, an anomaly, and do not derive from the evil intent of far-left radicals. They provide an incentive against flight without discriminating against the poor.

Trump seems unaware of how the courts work. He does not understand that those deemed at risk of committing subsequent crimes are not released, regardless of the kind of bail system in use. He does not understand that bail addresses flight risk, not risk to the community.

It is often said that "a little knowledge is dangerous." In this case, very little knowledge is very dangerous.

August 22, 2025
Trump Takes Over D.C. on a Whim
Dear Editors,

Conservative *New York Times* columnist David French wrote that President Trump sent troops into D.C. on a "whim."

French is correct. This was a whim induced by a carjacking. Crime in D.C. is still too high, but it is hard to call it an emergency situation when it is at a 30-year low, and no one considered it an emergency situation when it was higher. In fact, in a recent poll, 80 percent of D.C. residents opposed the federal intervention.

Putting more law enforcement personnel on the ground and demanding more arrests will surely lead to more arrests, although so far only approximately 550 have been arrested in almost two weeks, many of whom would have been arrested without federal troops involved, and some of whom will surely be released. Some were simply illegal immigrants without a criminal record, no threat to public safety at all.

We also learned that Attorney General Bondi instructed D.C. prosecutors to upgrade charges, to allege felonies in lieu of historically charged misdemeanors. And that a grand jury, which proverbially will indict a metaphorical ham sandwich, refused to indict a man charged with felony assault for throwing an actual ham sandwich at a law enforcement official. Obviously, Trump's main interest is driving up the number of arrests and escalating the severity of charges, all to allow him to claim great success.

Trump's other interest seems to be just making a show of force. Some of the National Guard have been patrolling tony Georgetown, monuments, the National Mall, and other tourist areas where there is almost no crime. Some have been assigned to clean up garbage.

Regardless, the most important point here is that however many arrests are ultimately made in D.C., or how few, if any, murders take place during the limited time D.C. has a federal law enforcement employee on nearly every corner, they will not be dispositive. There is a good reason the law allows federal intervention only for emergencies. In an emergency, a riot may be quelled, marauding gangs or rioters may be arrested; there is a tangible benefit to federal intervention. The law does not allow federal intervention merely for a high crime rate because the intervention is time-limited, unsustainable, and, therefore, ultimately inconsequential. When the feds leave D.C., no riots will have been quelled, no marauding gangs will have been contained, everything will revert to how it was. Nothing significant will have changed, certainly not in the long run. A band-aid will have been applied, and then removed.

The District of Columbia and American cities need solutions to chronic problems. A lasting effect on crime requires more funding, not less; it requires more law enforcement personnel, not less; and it requires addressing the root causes of crime. Trump has shown no interest in any of that.

Trump specializes in bombastic display. Patrol the streets for a month to great fanfare, join the patrol yourself for a photo op, then perhaps move on to another display in another city. Nothing significant accomplished, but that was never the point.

It is merely performative policing addressing an imagined emergency.

———————

August 23, 2025
Next Up: Chicago and African American Ladies With Red Hats
Dear Editors,

Now that President Trump's takeover of the District of Columbia is nearer to its end, he announced that Chicago was up next.

Trump introduced his planned Chicago takeover with an almost inexplicable comment, "The people in Chicago—they are wearing red hats, African American ladies, beautiful ladies, are saying, 'Please, President Trump, come to Chicago.'"

I suspect that African American ladies are thinking something else. Trump's long history of disrespect and ill-treatment of blacks is shameful. This goes back to the '70s when he and his father refused to rent apartments to blacks, and includes, among other things, his heinous racial profiling of the Central Park Five (eventually found innocent—Trump never issuing an apology), calling African nations "shithole countries," the fake Obama birther conspiracy which he touted for years, and hitting rock bottom with his response to Black Lives Matter.

No public figure in the United States demonstrated more antagonism to, less empathy for, and less support of the Black Lives Matter movement than Trump. Among other insults, he called it a "symbol of hate," referred to protesters as thugs, and, in one instance, directed law enforcement to dispel a peaceful racial protest outside the White House with tear gas, rubber bullets, and clubs, all to clear a path for a self-serving photo op.

His disdain of Black Lives Matter may have been the nadir in Trump's disrespect of blacks, but it was by no means the end. In just the last year, he eliminated references to slavery, racial segregation, brutal police killings, and other important features of Black American history from museums; he removed mention of black historical figures from the Arlington National Cemetery and the National Park Service websites; and he renamed Army bases after confederate generals, including ones who supported slavery.

Furthermore, black women have suffered a stunning loss of 319,000 jobs in just the first five months following Trump's reelection. This was partly due to their increased prevalence in agencies Elon Musk and Trump targeted, including the Department of Education, USAID, and the Internal Revenue Service, among others. But, also, the ACLU filed a complaint alleging that blacks were disproportionally affected by job losses as part of Trump's plan to undo hires purportedly related to DEI.

There is still more. Trump cut funding for Medicaid, for SNAP, for public education, for Historically Black Colleges and Universities, and eliminated DEI programs everywhere. These acts will have lasting consequences, none of them good for minorities.

As for combating crime, Trump cut $1 billion from the Department of Justice budget, which included programs supporting local law enforcement, cut funding for Community Oriented Policing Services and the ATF, and is trying to eliminate federal aid to Chicago and other blue cities, some of which would go to local law enforcement. Trump has actually hindered local efforts to battle crime. In this context, his Superman to the rescue act rings hollow.

Does Trump really think that African American women are not aghast at his attempt to whitewash slavery? And to whitewash other features of black history and accomplishments? And not aghast at his other indignities?

Not surprisingly, Trump received only 20 percent of the black vote in the 2024 presidential election.

I doubt those "beautiful African American ladies" abruptly changed course and are pining for Trump to come to Chicago for any reason, let alone for a self-aggrandizing show of power.

His boasting to the contrary aside, when it comes to African Americans, Trump has much to atone for.

—————————

August 28, 2025
Trump's Selective Agenda for Crime
Dear Editors,

Earlier this month, a deranged man shot more than 500 rounds into the Center for Disease Control and Prevention in Atlanta, killing a responding officer in the process. This incident has several aspects that characterize President Trump's selective interests in fighting crime.

First, why did Trump fail to comment on this shooting? In contrast, a single carjacking and assault in D.C. led to a federal takeover of the D.C. police department and deployment of the National Guard. Atlanta also has crime; it has been in and out of the top 10 cities for the highest murder rates over the last several years. In one case, Trump is silent; in the other, he goes ballistic.

Second, why did this shooter have access to weapons that could fire 500 rounds so quickly? In this particular incident, the weapons belonged to the shooter's father, but why does any civilian own weapons designed for mass killings? When will Trump and the Republican Party ever understand that nearly unfettered gun ownership results in homicides, that sensible gun control is sensible, and that the Second Amendment of the Constitution calls for "A well regulated militia," which suggests that guns should be well regulated. Gun proponents interpret that differently, but that seems strained and clearly self-serving. If the astute and meticulous authors of the Second Amendment intended guns as an exception to "well regulated," they would have said so.

Third, do RFK Jr. and Trump, as his sponsor, understand their role in this shooting? The gunman's motivation reportedly was his belief that he had been harmed by the COVID-19 vaccine, likely having heard RFK Jr.'s absurd proclamation that these vaccines were "the deadliest vaccines ever made." In the wake of this horror, both RFK Jr. and Trump should have made public comments specifying that the COVID-19 vaccine saved a huge number of lives, had few side effects, and that nobody should think or, especially, act on anything to the contrary. Their failure to do so is both irresponsible and dangerous.

Trump routinely portrays himself as a heroic crime-fighter. But prior to sending troops into D.C., he cut funds that would have gone to local policing, and he gutted the District Attorney's office of D.C. He sends, or threatens to send, federal troops only into areas politically less friendly to him, and not to Republican-run areas, even though some of them suffer from very high crime rates. His interventions are short-lived, and he has no agenda that targets root causes of crime or supports local law enforcement efforts.

Trump is not fighting an actual war on crime. He only has a selective agenda that serves his self-interests. Americans deserve much better.

———————

September 5, 2025
Donald Trump as "The Defunder in Chief"
Dear Editors,

President Trump's invasion of D.C. is now three weeks old. Trump has already declared it a great success, repeatedly citing the arrest total, now up to 1,800.

Has this really been a great success?

Actually, the number of arrests cited greatly overstates the impact of the incursion. The 995 arrests in the first two weeks of the surge were barely increased compared with 874 in the two weeks prior and reportedly similar to the number of arrests in the same time period one year ago. And many of the recent arrests were simply alleged firearms prosecutions, rather than, as originally intended, of people who had committed crimes and were on the loose. The facts tell a very different narrative than we hear from Trump and his representatives.

Furthermore, Trump directed his law enforcement personnel to lower the usual standards for an arrest and to hype up the charges (known as trumped-up charges). Thus, we have witnessed multiple grand juries refusing to return indictments, with some of the prosecution's cases being just awful. This predicts that more than the usual percentage of those arrested will be released back into the community.

On the other hand, the good news is that there has been a decrease in crimes committed in D.C. as compared to historical norms. A decrease in crime out of proportion to an increase in arrests suggests that the former is mostly due to the acute deterrent effect of the imposing law enforcement presence, rather than to the removal of criminals.

A decrease in crime for any reason is a good thing, but the D.C. incursion teaches nothing new. If you put more than two thousand national guardsmen into any city—metaphorically, a cop on every corner—the crime rate will fall. That was no Trump insight or accomplishment. Nor was it a real crime-fighting plan, since whenever the guardsmen leave, the situation will quickly return to baseline.

Still, the D.C. takeover did make a point, just not the point Trump intended or understands. If more law enforcement personnel out on the street reduces crime, as many studies have shown, and as happened in D.C., then an actual plan to combat crime should involve, well, placing more law enforcement personnel out on the street. It seems axiomatic. And do so permanently, not just for one or two months, and in all metropolitan areas, not just following the futile Trump one-at-a-time approach to the 350 cities in the U.S. with a population of 100,000 or more.

The teaching point from the D.C. experience is this: Train and hire more policemen. Which requires increased federal funding to cities for training and hiring more policemen.

Yet Trump did the opposite! "Defund the police" was perhaps the single worst thing the far-left ever proposed, but it was Donald Trump, the same man who vociferously decried that far-left slogan, who actually slashed police funding. When the smoke finally cleared, it turned out that Trump was the one who actually defunded the police. Per Lewis Carroll in Alice in Wonderland, "Up is down [...] down is up."

If Trump is sincere about fighting crime, his first step should be to reverse "defund the police" and endorse "re-fund the police." That is, to undo the damage that he has done to fighting crime in America.

PART FOUR

More Craziness

CHAPTER 17

MISCELLANEOUS

March 22, 2025
Trump at the NCAA Wrestling Finals? Why?
Dear Editors,

As a former college wrestler, I attended this weekend's NCAA Wrestling Championships along with a group of erstwhile teammates. Prior to the Finals, rumor seeped out, supported by the increased security, including roadblocks, a massive influx of security guards and numerous Secret Service agents, that President Trump was attending the matches.

At first, that seemed odd. Wrestling is not a popular spectator sport and competitions are attended almost exclusively by members of the wrestling community: ex-wrestlers (identified by body shape and cauliflower ears), families, girlfriends, and fellow competitors. Trump is not a member of that community. He was not a wrestler; no one in his inner crowd was a wrestler. He was not known to attend a single wrestling match all year. So why was he there, seemingly out of the blue?

The answer became obvious when Trump strolled in gleefully to a standing ovation. Wrestling is most popular in the rural Midwest, which births much of the wrestling community. This was a predictably very pro-Trump crowd. He was guaranteed an ovation. That is why he showed up.

Trump then sat in a seat on the floor, by chance, directly in my line of sight. He showed virtually no interest in the matches, mostly keeping his head down, occasionally chatting with his sidekick Elon Musk. That changed abruptly when any of the newly crowned (midwestern, rural) champions strode toward him for a handshake and photo op. Trump became newly energized, jumping to his feet with the requisite big grin. Then went back to half-asleep.

Turns out, the president of the United States actually took a road trip, an evening out of his presidential schedule, for the sole purpose of enjoying a standing ovation from a group of strangers.

———————

July 5, 2025
Trump Cites Shylock
Dear Editors,

Yesterday, in celebrating the passage of his bill, Trump cited "Shylock and bad people."

Shylock was the Jewish moneylender in Shakespeare's *Merchant of Venice* known for his penurious ways, famously asking for a "pound of flesh." Shylock has long been used as an anti-Semitic prototype, decrying an alleged excessive frugality and heartless nature of Jews in financial matters.

Trump was amply criticized for using this anti-Semitic term.

I give Trump some leeway here. This comment was clearly spur-of-the-moment, probably without malice. But, also, not a surprise, nothing new, and not irrelevant. Trump's response was lost in the hysteria of the anti-Semitism charge, but still telling. Instead of saying "oops, my bad, I forgot, I am sorry," he very likely lied, claiming not to know Shylock was a Jewish slur. Trump describes himself as highly intelligent, a "stable genius." He is an educated man with a Jewish daughter, son-in-law, and grandchildren. He has had many personal, business, and political Jewish acquaintances, partners, and friends over his 79 years. It is hard to imagine that he was not familiar with the Shylock slur.

Which leads to: What does Trump really think of Jews?

On one hand, he projects himself as strongly pro-Israel; he is very popular in Israel and increasingly popular with American Jews. His share of the Jewish vote increased from 24 to 32 percent over his three elections.

However, pro-Israel is not the exact same thing as pro-Jewish, any more than anti-Israel is the same as anti-Semitic. A pro-Israel stance might simply be to Trump's political benefit at this point in time.

Actually, there is ample evidence that Trump's stance toward Jews is not so favorable. For instance, spontaneous utterances tend to reflect someone's basic beliefs and inclinations; the utterances are not arbitrary or random. So, the Shylock comment should not be dismissed offhand.

Further, the Shylock comment is consistent with much that should give Jews pause. Here is a partial list:

—It is of the same ilk as imagery he has used of several Jews, including philanthropist George Soros, chairman of the Federal Reserve Janet Yellen, and Goldman Sachs CEO Lloyd Blankfein, as background support in discussions about undue control of national and international financial systems.

—Similarly, he told a Jewish audience in 2019 that "A lot of you are in the real estate business, because I know you very well. You are brutal killers, not nice people at all."

—He commented "there were very fine people on both sides" in the 2017 Charlottesville march that featured white supremacists chanting "Jews will not replace us."

—He entertained the overtly anti-Semitic Kanye West and the white nationalist, Holocaust denier Nick Fuentes at Mar-a-Lago.

—He embraced and introduced a slew of people into government known for making anti-Semitic comments or gestures or having associations with overt anti-Semites, including Elon Musk, Kash Patel, RFK Jr. ("Jews engineered COVID-19"), Kingsley Wilson, and others.

—He has been quoted by his former chief of staff John Kelly as saying, "Hitler did some good things too," and admiring German generals.

—In a 1990 interview he said that he kept a copy of Hitler's *Mein Kampf*, and his ex-wife Ivana said he kept some of Hitler's speeches at his bedside.

It is hard to know for sure, but it is easy to conclude from the above that Trump holds some core anti-Semitic beliefs—particularly the Shylock canard—and that any favorable Jewish or pro-Israel comments or actions owe not to an intrinsic pro-Jewish sentiment, but to his usual transactional behavior and political calculus. When the interests of both parties align, he behaves one way, and if and when they diverge, he will behave another.

In summary, Jews should not dismiss yesterday's Shylock reference. It comes from a deep place.

————————

July 19, 2025
The Re-renaming of Confederate Army Bases: As If We Are All Idiots
Dear Editors,

During the Biden administration, the Department of Defense renamed Fort Bragg and eight other Army bases previously named for Confederate generals and soldiers, and in the process honored Black soldiers, a U.S. president, and trailblazing women. It seemed quite reasonable, as it is long past time to stop celebrating folks who favored slavery, owned slaves, fought for secession, and stood against the Republic.

This idea was affirmed with the overwhelming bipartisan passage—86-8 in the Senate, 377-48 in the House—of the 2020 National Defense Authorization Act. President Trump vetoed it late in his first term, one of the few people around against it, but his veto was easily overridden, a powerful bipartisan rebuke to his peculiar opposition.

The removal of the Confederate names did not seem to create too much of a stir until Trump announced, after his reelection, that he would change the names back. It is doubtful that Trump is fond of the Confederacy—that would be really too weird—but some of the forts had been renamed after blacks and women, and Trump ascribes that to the DEI movement, Black Lives Matter, and "woke-ness," all of which he detests.

Earlier this year, Trump, along with marionette Defense Secretary Pete Hegseth, re-renamed two forts. That took on a pathetic aura when they brought back the original surnames, as they said they would, but then claimed that the surnames referred to different individuals than the original honorees, pretending that they were not paying homage to the Confederacy. Do they think that we are all idiots?

Recently, Trump announced the remaining seven name changes were on the way. No news yet on whether he will do the same deception as earlier.

I do not think the names of these Army bases are as important as the bigger issue about DEI, and Trump's relentless attack on it, this being just one very public and concrete example.

No reasonable person is against diversity or equality or inclusion. These are basic characteristics of decent and fair-minded thinking, as taught in religious venues, schools, and households around the world. When people, excluding committed bigots, say they are against DEI, I assume they mean to say that they are against the excesses of the DEI movement, which are sometimes totally excessive—for example, "defund the police"—but not against DEI per se.

It is not surprising that the DEI movement went overboard in some of its actions and sayings. That is common to new movements, particularly in volatile areas (think of the anti-Vietnam War riots). These initial extremes usually elicit counter-responses, and the counter-responses often go too far as well. The point-counterpoint ideally ends up with a common sense compromise. This dialectic process, often referred to as "thesis-antithesis-synthesis," has been around since the ancient Greeks all the way up to the nineteenth century philosophers Hegel and Kant.

However, the Trump and Republican responses to DEI—whitewashing words, denying the transgender identity, eliminating officers, positions, programs, grants and contracts, the comic-pathetic re-renaming of Army bases to re-honor the Confederacy—is so far out there and the hatred so palpable that it is hard to envision a synthesis ever being reached. To find a compromise you need at least some common ground, some recognition and respect of the other side, and that seems absent here.

That is sad because the history of these processes predicted that eventually we would reap the benefits of DEI without its absurd overreach. Maybe there is still hope for that, but not with Trump fighting a war against tolerance, a monomaniacal battle bucking the arc of history toward accepting and integrating new ideas and other people not exactly like yourself.

Back in 2020, a more independent Republican Party overrode Trump's mania on this Army base naming issue. But five years later, his intimidated party is in complete obeisance to whatever he wants.

One Republican, Rep. Don Bacon of Nebraska, did call the re-renamings "stupid as hell." But he is a singular voice on a deserted island. And he probably stands there only because he is not running for reelection and is relatively immune from Trump's usual intimidation.

With Trump taking the extreme and uncompromising position that diversity is evil, equality is evil, and inclusion is evil—as bizarre as all that sounds—"synthesis" has left town.

———————

August 28, 2025
The Proud Boys and Oath Keepers: Standing Down on Their Own
Dear Editors,

In the Trump-Biden presidential debate in September 2020, President Trump famously refused to criticize the white supremacist group called the Proud Boys. Instead, he told them to "stand back and stand down." In essence, Trump told this noxious group to stay quiet pending further instructions from him, which suggested solidarity, shared priorities, and goals.

The comment received such widespread condemnation, including from Republicans, that the next day, in an obvious fabrication, Trump said that he did not even know who the Proud Boys were. Such was the sorry state of that extremist group at the time—Trump was forced to publicly disown them, albeit as a pretense.

Shortly afterwards, the Proud Boys disgraced themselves by standing forward and standing up, at Trump's prodding, in the attempted insurrection on Jan. 6. Their leader, Enrique Tarrio, was subsequently sentenced to 22 years in prison. Stewart Rhodes, the leader of a similar white supremacist group, the militia-style Oath Keepers, also went to prison. Dozens of followers of Tarrio or Rhodes were also imprisoned. Both organizations seemed dead in the water.

But [...] what a comeback! Immediately after reelection in 2024, Trump pardoned all those sentenced for Jan. 6 related crimes, referred to them as great patriots, and released them for further duty.

Then, oddly, both the Proud Boys and the Oath Keepers seemed to drop out of sight. Neither lead demonstrations anymore. Rhodes is nowhere to be seen and Tarrio mostly just does podcasts. They have gone quiet.

It would be nice if that was due to widespread repudiation by American society, or its opposite, some new rational thinking on their part.

Unfortunately, neither is the case. Proud Boys leader Tarrio provided the actual explanation, saying that "Things we were doing and talking about in 2017 that were taboo, they are no longer taboo—they're mainstream now." Even more tellingly, he added, "Honestly, what do we have to complain about these days?" His message was that Trump has been so in sync with the Proud Boys' agenda that they no longer have anything to do. The same is true with the Oath Keepers. Their *raison d'être* has disappeared. Mission accomplished, via Trump!

There might be no more damning statement about Trump's second term to date than that the Proud Boys and Oath Keepers are so pleased with everything that he has done that they have voluntarily, without prompting this time, stepped back and stood down.

—————————

September 6, 2025
The Limitations of Parental Control
Dear Editors,

Florida surgeon general Joseph Ladapo, in conjunction with Governor Ron DeSantis, announced that Florida would be the first state to end school vaccine mandates. Dr. Ladapo, with no hesitation regarding either hyperbole or histrionics, stated that mandatory vaccines were "immoral" and akin to "slavery." He seemed curiously unaware that he was accusing 49 other state governments of being immoral and engaging in slavery for over 40 years.

This followed President Trump's previous executive order banning the COVID-19 vaccine mandate in schools.

Following Trump's lead, DeSantis and Ladapo stated that only parents can make decisions for their children. Infants and children up to a certain age cannot make informed decisions for themselves, need a surrogate decision-maker, and, of course, parents should primarily fill that role. But is that concept inviolate? Has it ever been? Specifically, what happens when parents make bad, perhaps horrible, decisions for their children?

That happens, for example, when parents do not provide adequate food, shelter, hygiene, safety, or education. If parental neglect or mistreatment is bad enough, the children may be removed from their parents, and parents can even be convicted of child abuse. In those instances, by societal decree, we have given the state the right to intervene in the interests of protecting children. So, clearly, "only parents decide" is not the inviolate law that Ladapo and DeSantis suggested. It is not the 11th commandment!

Children are born into a world with many infectious diseases that, throughout history, have caused severe illnesses and deaths. Fortunately, we now have safe and effective vaccines that provide substantial protection. When a parent decides to withhold these potentially lifesaving vaccines from a child, he or she is abrogating his responsibility to protect that child and putting that child at unnecessary risk. It would be entirely consistent with our national ethos for someone to step in and protect the child; in this case, it would be the rest of us, via our endorsement of mandatory childhood vaccines.

Parental control over children has always been limited by common sense and society's wish to protect the well-being of children. That seems to have escaped Trump, DeSantis, and Ladapo, who wrongly think of parental control as an inviolate moral law.

————————

September 7, 2025
The One-Sided Supreme Court
Dear Editors,

President Trump just had a horrible week in court, with nearly his entire agenda eviscerated by multiple adverse rulings. Consider:

—A federal appeals court ruled that the majority of his tariffs exceeded the limits of his constitutional powers. That is a huge part of his economic plan.
—His mass deportation policy was set back by a Court of Appeals ruling that disallowed his removal of alleged Venezuelan gang members based on his improper "use of a wartime statute during peacetime."
—Related, a federal judge ruled that Homeland Security secretary Kristi Noem exceeded her authority when she terminated the Temporary Protected Status that covered hundreds of thousands of Haitians and Venezuelans.
—A U.S. district judge ruled that Trump's deployment of the National Guard and Marines to Los Angeles had been illegal, which, if upheld, will eviscerate his war on crime.
—A U.S. federal court overturned billions in funding cuts to Harvard University on the basis that they violated the college's free speech rights. This will cripple Trump's war on universities.

Wow! Imagine your economic plan, deportation plan, crime plan, and crippling of universities plan all invalidated in one week. That is nearly Trump's entire agenda.

Yet Trump seemed relatively unperturbed. That is because he has a backup plan, to appeal everything to the Supreme Court, where he has had great success. Most importantly, among other actions, the Court purposefully stalled its ruling on his Jan. 6 indictments, allowing the 2024 election to make them moot (the Court likely kept him out of jail); it then gave him near-complete immunity from prosecution, as they say, (nearly) above the law. It has also frequently used its shadow docket for emergency motions to halt, with little to no explanation, lower court rulings that called various Trump actions illegal or unconstitutional.

The many decisions favorable to Trump have been decided along party lines.[1] Everyone knows that with a differently constituted Court the rulings would

1 The Supreme Court just ruled that federal agents in Los Angeles could stop and question civilians based on their Latin appearance or language, or type of employment. A federal judge had previously ruled that this constituted racial profiling and violated the Fourth Amendment. Justice Kavanaugh, in explaining the Supreme Court's decision, wrote that we should trust the judgment of federal agents as to what determines reasonable suspicion

have been the exact opposite. It makes absolutely no sense for critical judicial rulings to be so conditional. It completely undermines any faith in the Court, and that is reflected in recent polling which revealed that the Court's approval rating is at an all-time low. That is not just a popularity contest; it reflects public belief that the highest court in the land is not necessarily deciding cases solely on their merits.

How did we get to this situation and what can we do about it?

The one-sided composition of today's Supreme Court—so favorable to Trump—was partly historical happenstance, but also owed to Mitch McConnell's dishonesty. As Senate Majority Leader, McConnell blocked President Obama from selecting a justice based upon the unprecedented and tortured reasoning that it was "too late" in Obama's term—"too late" as arbitrarily decided by McConnell. Subsequently, in an overt act of hypocrisy, he allowed President Trump his own appointment at an even later time in his term. This resulted in a 6-3 conservative majority, rather than 5-4. That may not seem like much of a difference, but in some cases, a 5-4 composition would allow for just a single wavering conservative justice to change the outcome. And might even lead to a 5-4 liberal lean with the next justice's departure, rather than face decades of the same imbalance.

I doubt the Founders ever imagined that one person would stoop as low as McConnell, or realized that a single person, one senator, could mold the court for decades solely in the interest of advancing his party's views. Or that an imbalanced Court such as we have now would give a president like Trump almost unlimited power. If they did imagine those possibilities, they would have devised a different system in order to prevent all of that. A system in which decisions would be free of political bias. A system in which the structure of the court could not be engineered to repetitively support a particular political agenda. That would be best for Democrats and Republicans, for all of us.

---

and that wrongful detainment and the requirement to carry proof of citizenship are just minor inconveniences. Justice Sotomayor dissented, calling this "unconscionably irreconcilable with our nation's constitutional guarantees." That is what you call a difference of opinion! Not surprisingly, the federal judge and the three dissenting Supreme Court justices are all Democrats, and the six justices in the majority are all Republicans—a perfect 10 for 10 in terms of adhering to political leanings. That cannot be good for America.

Can we correct that? Is a different system still possible? Is there a nonpartisan solution in the interests of fairness and the common good, rather than just winning at all costs?

I say, "yes," and here it is:

Expand the Supreme Court to 15 jurists. Six will always be appointed by the highest ranking Republican, six by the highest ranking Democrat, and three will require majority approval of those 12 appointees. Whenever a seat becomes open, it will be filled in a manner to maintain that ratio, no matter who the president is at that time. That would mean that even if both parties appointed six extreme ideologues, cases would still be decided by three sensible, mainstream justices agreed upon by both sides.

On what basis could one object to that? Does anyone have a better idea? Why is it in the public interest for either party to ever have a majority? Does it benefit the Republic as the judicial pendulum perpetually swings from liberal to conservative, and back again, ad nauseam?

———————

September 24, 2025
An Apt Ending: Stark Raving Mad and Embarrassing
Dear Readers,

President Trump just addressed the UN with an unprecedented series of self-aggrandizing and egotistical confabulations while, at the same time, belittling the rest of the world.

Among other comments, Trump stated that "We are the hottest country anywhere in the world and there is no country even close […] in my first term, I built the greatest economy in the history of the world […] but this time it is actually much bigger and even better […]. America is respected again like it has never been respected before […]. I have ended seven unendable wars. There's never been anything like that […] everyone says that I should get the Nobel Peace Prize […]. I've been right about everything […]."

If anyone in my family ever spoke like that, I would break into tears and have that person in a psychiatrist's office the next day.

Trump's comments got even weirder.

He ascribed a momentarily stalled escalator to a nefarious UN plot against him. Lunacy begetting lunacy, White House press secretary Caroline Leavitt agreed that "it looked like sabotage," and Senator Mike Lee (R-UT)—you cannot make this up—called for defunding the UN for "orchestrating escalator and teleprompter malfunctions."

Combining the stalled escalator with transient teleprompter and audio problems, Trump called it "three very sinister events [...] triple sabotage at the UN," and demanded an investigation. He appeared to be serious.

Quite apropos, journalist Ishaan Tharoor reported that a senior foreign diplomat at the UN texted him that "Trump is stark raving mad. Do Americans not see how embarrassing this is?"

Every American, regardless of political interests, should be embarrassed that our president, his press secretary, and a U.S. senator all believe that the United Nations sabotaged an escalator in an attempt to injure the president. This is comic book material.

Trump's delusions of grandeur, megalomania, paranoia, and disdain for others, all on display in one setting, captured the essence of his psyche and the manner in which he has served as president. His behavior at the UN provides an apt summary of, and ending to, this book.

AFTERWORD

As I look back on this book, one theme stands out. My objections to things Trump said and did were not limited to simple disagreements, policy differences, his disrespect for, and ill-treatment of, people, his ego-mania, or his unprecedented quest for power at the expense of our democracy. Worse than that, some of Trump's actions have led to deaths, and he is still doing things that, unless reversed, will cause more people to die.

His bungling of the COVID-19 pandemic is the most obvious and largest cause of unnecessary deaths to date, but may end up far surpassed by his slashing of support for HIV care and other health-related conditions in Africa. Additional Trump actions that have had or will have deadly consequences include the loss of Medicaid and health care for millions, the destruction of contraceptives meant for Africa, the gutting of FEMA, the war on the environment, the war on vaccines, science, and health care, the deportations of immigrants to jails with inhumane conditions or in dangerous countries, his timid response to Putin's war on Ukraine, and his support of Netanyahu's excesses in Gaza. All of that is considered unforgivable by many of us.

The resistance to Trump will continue until the end of his term. The goal is realistic—he is not going to be removed by impeachment, he is not going away, he is not going to change even one iota. But we can, if we continue with persistent fervor, if we recruit like-minded folks to the cause, perhaps act as a brake, a sea anchor of sorts. That is my goal: to provide impetus and spark for others in this battle to keep fighting, even to up their games, in an attempt to collectively limit Trump's damage to our country.

But this book ends here, even with several years remaining in Trump's term. There are two reasons for this. First, it is now long enough to have made its point. Second, the value of the book plummets if it waits until Trump leaves office. At that time, the war against Trump becomes moot. Released now, with Trump still in office, perhaps I can accomplish some good. Fingers crossed.

www.ingramcontent.com/pod-product-compliance
Lightning Source LLC
Chambersburg PA
CBHW022355280326
41935CB00007B/193

* 9 7 8 1 8 3 9 9 9 9 4 9 9 *